30 Days of Sex Talks
Empowering Your Child with Knowledge of Sexual Intimacy
For Ages 8-11
Second Edition

Educate and Empower Kids, LLC
© 2023 by Educate and Empower Kids

All rights reserved. Published 2023.

ISBN: 978-1-7367215-8-2

The paper used in this publication meets the minimum requirements of the American National Standard for Information Sciences—Permanence of Paper for Printed Library Materials, ANSI Z39.48-1992.

IF YOU ENJOYED THIS BOOK,
PLEASE LEAVE A POSITIVE REVIEW ON AMAZON.COM

Thank you to the following people for their support of our 30 Days of Sex Talks projects
Ed Allison
Mary Ann Benson, MSW, LSW
Scott Hounsell
Cliff Park

For great resources and information, follow us.

Facebook: www.facebook.com/educateempowerkids
Twitter: @EduEmpowerKids
Pinterest: @EmpowerLDSKids
Instagram: @EduEmpowerKids
www.educateempowerkids.org

Be sure to check out our accompanying video series for this book at educateempowerkids.org

To view or download the additional resources listed at the end of each lesson, please follow the link in this QR code.

Educate and Empower Kids would like to acknowledge the following people who contributed time, talents, and energy to this publication:

Dina Alexander, MS

Amanda Scott
Miriam Foulke
Jenny Webb, MA
Caron C. Andrews
K. Parker

Design and Illustration by:
Jera Mehrdad and Zachary Hourigan

30 Days of Sex Talks

Empowering Your Child with Knowledge of Sexual Intimacy

For AGES 8-11

30 DAYS OF SEX TALKS
TABLE OF CONTENTS

INTRODUCTION ... x

AGE 8-11

1. Public vs. Private ... 1
2. Male Anatomy ... 5
3. Female Anatomy ... 7
4. Puberty for Boys ... 9
5. Puberty for Girls ... 11
6. Menstrual Cycle ... 13
7. Physical Mechanics of Sexual Intercourse ... 15
8. Emotional Aspects of Sex ... 19
9. Relationships Are Good and Wonderful ... 21
10. What Does a Healthy Relationship Look Like? ... 23
11. Romantic Love ... 25
12. Different Kinds of Families ... 27
13. Gender & Gender Roles ... 29
14. Sexual Identification ... 31
15. Ready for a Sexual Relationship ... 33
16. Curiosity ... 35
17. Masturbation ... 37
18. Children Do Not Have Sex ... 41
19. What to Do if Something Has Happened to You – Who to Talk To ... 43
20. How Predators Groom Children ... 45
21. How to Say No ... 47
22. Your Instincts Keep You Safe ... 49
23. Pornography ... 51
24. Sexting & Social Media ... 53
25. Being Media Savvy ... 55
26. Body Image ... 57
27. Self-worth & Self-esteem ... 61
28. Shame and Guilt ... 63
29. Pregnancy ... 65
30. STDs and STIs ... 67
Topic Cards ... 70

GLOSSARY ... 80

"Parenthood is about raising and celebrating the child you have, not the child you thought you'd have. It's about understanding your child is exactly the person they are supposed to be. And, if you're lucky, they might be the teacher who turns you into the person you're supposed to be."

—UNKNOWN

INTRODUCTION

Dear Parents and Guardians,

You and I both know that the most important work we will ever do on earth is to teach our children to be kind, intelligent people. Our homes are the first and most important schoolroom our children will have. This makes it the perfect place to have deep, meaningful conversations about important topics like love, healthy relationships, marriage, sexual intimacy, and the dangers that threaten their future happiness.

We are living in complicated and uncertain times. Our kids are surrounded by unhealthy or false messages about their bodies, relationships, and human sexuality, and it is our job to teach them what is true and what is not. It is vital that we begin these discussions to help them understand what healthy sexuality is, how special their bodies are, AND that they can come to us as parents to find answers to questions.

With this pragmatic, easy-to-use program, you will find many opportunities to start conversations about these essential topics. In addition, using these lessons will help you create an environment in your home which encourages open discussions about many other topics that come up as you are raising your child.

WHAT'S INCLUDED

This curriculum includes 30 simple, yet meaningful lessons, insightful directions, and an extensive glossary of over 130 terms to help you. Each lesson includes introductory points to consider, critical teaching information, powerful discussion questions, and additional resources to enrich your family's learning experience. Some topics even have an accompanying activity or song to inspire further conversation.

PREPARING FOR SUCCESS

- Consider your individual child's age, developmental stage, and personality in conjunction with each topic, as well as your family's values and individual situation. These will help you adapt the material in order to produce the best discussion. It's important that you begin your daily talks with just one topic in mind and that you make every experience, however brief, truly meaningful.

If you feel like your child isn't ready to discuss the bullets listed under the topic or if you feel that your child's knowledge is more advanced, please note that we have also developed this curriculum for other age groups and it is available for purchase. It's important to discuss things with your child based on their own maturity level; progressing or referring back at your own pace.

If you are positive and real with your child when it comes to talking about sexual intimacy, they will learn that you are available not just for this conversation, but for ANY discussion.

- Plan ahead of time but don't create an event. Having a plan or planning ahead of time will remove much of the awkwardness you might feel in talking about these subjects with your child. In not creating an event, you are making the discussions feel more spontaneous, the experience more repeatable, and yourself more approachable.

- Please know, you do not need to be an expert to have purposeful, informative discussions with your kids. In fact, we feel strongly that leaning on your own personal experiences—both mistakes and successes—is a great way to use life lessons to teach your child. If done properly, these talks will bring you closer to your child than you could have ever imagined.

You know and love your child more than anyone, so you decide when and where these discussions take place. In time, you will recognize and enjoy teaching moments in everyday life with your child.

NEED TO KNOW

- This program is meant to be simple! It's organized into simple topics with bullet points to be straightforward and create conversations. Each lesson may only take 10 minutes, but allow more time for your kids' questions and extra family discussion.

- This curriculum is not a one-discussion-fits-all. You guide the conversation and lead the discussion according to your unique situation. If you have three children, you will likely have three different conversations about the same topic.

- No program can cover all aspects of sexual intimacy perfectly for every individual circumstance. You can empower yourself with the knowledge you gain from this program to share with your child what you feel is the most important.

INSTRUCTIONS

BE POSITIVE

Take the fear and shame out of these discussions. Sex is natural and wondrous, and your child should feel nothing but positivity about it from you. If you do feel awkward, stay calm and use matter-of-fact tones in your discussions. It's easier than you think–just open your mouth and begin! It will get easier with every talk you have. Even after just a few talks, both you and your child will begin to look forward to this time you are spending together. Use experiences from your own life to begin a discussion if it makes you feel more comfortable. We have listed some tough topics here, but they are all discussed in a positive, informative way. Don't worry, you've got this!

ANSWER YOUR CHILD'S QUESTIONS

If you are embarrassed by your child's curiosity and questions, you're implying that there is something shameful about these topics. However, if you can answer those questions calmly and honestly, you're demonstrating that sexuality is positive, and that healthy relationships are something to look forward to when the time is right. Be sure to answer your child's questions practically and cheerfully and your child will learn that you are available not just for this discussion, but for any discussion. It's okay if you don't have all the answers, just tell them you will look for the answers and get back to them.

Create a Safe Zone

We recommend that you create a "safe zone" with your child and within your home. During the course of these conversations, your child should feel safe and free to ask any questions or make any comments without judgment or repercussions.

Your child should be able to use the term "safe zone" again and again to discuss, confide, and consult with you about the tough subjects they will be confronted with throughout life. It's highly recommended that, whenever possible, all parenting parties be involved in these discussions.

FOCUS ON INTIMACY

Help your child understand how incredible and uniting sex can be. Don't just talk about the mechanics of sex. Spend a significant amount of time talking about the beauty of love and sex, the reality of human relationships and how they are built and maintained. Children are continually exposed to examples of harmful relationships in the media. Many of them are teaching your child lessons about sexuality and interactions between people that are misleading, incomplete, or purely unhealthy. Real emotional intimacy is rarely portrayed, so it's your job to teach and model what true intimacy actually is. Your child needs you to help connect the dots between healthy relationships and sexuality. Model positive ways for your child to care for and appreciate his or her body, and how to protect, have a positive attitude toward, and make favorable choices for that body.

> Taking the time to talk about these topics will reiterate to your child how important they are to you.

BE THE SOURCE

Remember, you direct the conversations. Bring up the lesson points and questions that you feel are most important and allow the conversation to flow from there. You love and know your child better than anyone else, so you are the best person to judge what will be most effective. Pause and take into account your personal values, your beliefs, individual personalities, and family dynamics. You, the parent, can and should be the best source of information about sex and intimacy for your child. If you don't discuss these topics, your child will look for answers from other, less reliable and sometimes harmful sources like the internet, various media, and other kids.

It may feel a little strange at first, and there will be times when you doubt your wisdom and knowledge. But as you begin communicating with your child about these important topics, you will find the right words and this process will help you grow closer to your child. Never underestimate the power and influence you have with your children! They need you and they need your wisdom.

Dina Alexander
Educate and Empower Kids

Let's Get Started!

What a fun age this is! It is within this age group that children become much more aware of their bodies, the opposite gender, and the world around them. Knowledge about how the human body works, how your child's body is going to change, and how they can be ready for these changes will empower them. This age is also when children begin to have feelings of self-consciousness, being attracted to others, and general awareness of sexuality. This is why it's important to discuss relationships, body image, media, gender, masturbation, pornography, and protective information as well.

Remember, this program is meant to inspire conversations that we hope assist you in fostering an environment where difficult discussions are made easier. Enjoy this time with your kids. Take advantage of the one-on-one time these conversations will facilitate to become more comfortable talking with your child and to strengthen your bond further.

1. Public vs. Private

One of the most important things that parents can do is ensure their children know that the home is a "Safe Zone." The home should be a place where curiosity is encouraged and children feel comfortable coming to their parents with any and all questions they have. Parents can start these conversations by asking their children if they have questions about anything (sex, their bodies, pornography, or other topics). Discuss the "Safe Zone" mentioned in the introduction and remind your kids that they can ask you any question at any time, even ones that they think are strange, private, embarrassing, or "bad." If a child feels comfortable enough to go to their parents with questions, they're less likely to google a term they heard at school and face the full, uncensored onslaught that a search engine will provide.

Parents typically discuss various aspects of sexuality with their children at different ages. Help your kids understand that there's new information every child needs to hear at different stages in his or her life. As they grow older, you'll teach them more in-depth about whatever questions they have.

Start the Conversation

Explain to your child that those they socialize with (friends, siblings, classmates) might not be ready to talk about subjects like sex and puberty and those subjects should only be discussed with parents to avoid confusion. Always make sure to explain your reasoning. Children are very curious, and if the only answer to their questions is something along the lines of "You don't need to know about that right now, trust me" or "Drop the subject, I'm your parent," it's likely that their curiosity won't be satisfied. They could potentially go to other sources for answers to their questions. Try saying something like this instead: "Some people are uncomfortable talking about sex. Small children are at a different level of

 PUBLIC: *Belonging to or for the use of all people in a specific area, or all people as a whole. Something that is public is common, shared, collective, communal, and widespread.*

understanding and aren't ready to hear about the same things that others are yet. Sex isn't something to be discussed amongst children."

Explain to your child that there are times when it's okay to talk openly about one's thoughts, and times when it isn't appropriate to do so. Discuss with your child different times when it's appropriate to ask questions and share personal experiences and stories, and times when it is inappropriate to do so. For example, in a public setting when your child is around strangers, it's not a good idea to share a lot of personal information or stories, though it would be okay to share personal stories at home with their parents.

Questions for Your Child

- Why are some topics private? Why don't we talk about certain topics in public?
- Is it okay for an adult other than your parents to discuss sex with you?
- What are some things we can talk about in public with our friends?
- What are other topics that we consider public information?

   Note: This is a great time to talk about internet use and what information we can freely share publicly vs. what information isn't safe to share. Consider discussing the following list: full name, school, address, hobbies, phone number, medical history,

- *location, grades, parent's location, income, interests, etc.*
- What information is private and shouldn't be shared?

    Note: At this age, it is important to not only focus on activities that one does in private but also what conversations one has. We speak privately about sex, medical issues, and beliefs, while it's okay to talk about school, friends, and hobbies openly.

- Who should you discuss important private matters with?

    Note: This is a great time to revisit the topic of "stranger danger" with your child. If anyone, in-person or on the internet, asks questions about matters you agree are private, then ensure your child knows to come to you.

- Have you and your friends ever talked about sex?
- Why is it not a good idea to talk to other kids about sex?

Sample Dialogue

Parent: Is there anything that would seem strange to talk about in public?
(Allow your child to answer.)

Parent: Why would that seem strange to talk about in public?
(Allow your child to answer.)

Parent: It is important that we are aware of what we are sharing, where we are sharing it, and how what we are sharing could be received by others... Do you understand?
(Allow your child to answer.)

Additional Resources:

"Bodily Integrity: Teaching Your Child to Make the Best Choices for His or Her Body" from Educate and Empower Kids
This article offers parents a variety of tips on how they can teach their children to love and respect their own bodies in a culture that would demand otherwise.

"Talking to Kids About Public vs. Private Discussions" from Educate and Empower Kids
This article offers parents with statistics and perspectives from people who learned about private matters from their friends and wished they had learned from their parents instead.

"Modesty and Smart Clothing Choices: Teaching Our Kids to Be Seen for Who They Are" from Educate and Empower Kids
This article helps to educate kids on what modesty means so that they're able to make smart, context-appropriate clothing choices that will empower them through a combination of self-respect and self-confidence.

"The most important work you and I will ever do will be within the walls of our own homes."

—HAROLD B. LEE

2. Male Anatomy

There are societal expectations for the "desired" male form. There can be peer pressure with boys just starting puberty because they may feel like they won't ever get out of puberty. They may be at that age when they're starting to like girls more, and it's possible that changes from puberty could make them feel that they will never look like a man a woman could want. In creating a safe space in your home, your son can feel comfortable coming to you about his feelings. Assure him that he just needs to be him. Teach him to embrace his body, and it will help to alleviate those fears. It's important to teach your children that their bodies will never be perfect. And that's okay. It's beautiful anyway. Many older boys and girls struggle with their own body issues and body expectations of others, and teaching your child to be comfortable with their own bodies can help to lessen those struggles.

Teaching your son(s) the proper names for their male sexual organs can help to make them feel secure in their own bodies. Just as with their arms and legs, their sexual organs serve a purpose, and it's important for them to know about that purpose. The male body is anatomically different from the female body. It is a part of their identity. Use the glossary to help you discuss male anatomy (penis, testicle/scrotum, anus) with your child.

SCROTUM: *The pouch of skin underneath the penis that contains the testicles.*

Start the Conversation

Teach your child that sexual organs are the most fundamental way that boys and girls are different. Explain that a doctor or nurse can look at a baby and know the sex of that baby. Discuss the purpose of the penis and scrotum—urination and ejaculation of sperm. (See the glossary for terms and explanations.) Explain how the penis and scrotum can expand and contract with body temperature. Feel free to discuss foreskin, circumcision and your decision to circumcise or not.

If you have a diagram, now is a good time to use it. Talk about the breasts and nipples and how, even in men, nipples can be tender. Describe how nipples can be many shapes, sizes, and colors. Asking your child if they have heard any slang terms is a good way to gauge if they have been talking about or hearing about sex outside your home.

Questions for Your Child

- What are some things that make boys and girls physically different?
- What are some things that make boys and girls physically similar?
- What parts do you have? What parts does the opposite sex have?
- Men and women need each other! How do men and women compliment each other physically and emotionally?
- We have talked about the medically correct terms for these body parts, but there are many slang terms as well. What are some you have heard?
- People sometimes make jokes about body parts, especially our sex organs. This is the wrong attitude to have towards our bodies. Why are our sex organs special and private?
- What questions do you have about your body?

Sample Dialogue

Parent: Our bodies are all unique. Everyone shares body parts particular to their gender. Do you have any questions about your body? A particular part of your body? *(Allow your child to answer.)* Remind your child that they should use the proper names for all parts of the body.

Parent: I am here to help and to explain anything about your body. Please come to me if you have any more questions, okay?

Additional Resources:

"Why the Best Way to Protect Our Children is to Prepare Them" from Educate and Empower Kids
A sad, but real, truth is that there is a lot of bad in this world. The best thing you can do for your child is prepare them to better handle the bad, so they can enjoy the good.

"My Boys and Body Image: How Can I Help?" from Educate and Empower Kids
It's important to help protect your sons against the dangers of body issues; they are just as susceptible as girls are to distorted body views.

"How Teaching Healthy Sexuality Can Help Your Child Against the Predator, the Pressuring Partner, and the Prude" from Educate and Empower Kids
This article succinctly gives tips on how to empower your kids against the danger that can come from 3 different directions.

3. Female Anatomy

The physical changes that your daughter's body is going to go through will be far more visible than a boy's. There is a lot of pressure that can come from those around your daughter that can make her feel that these changes (or lack of) are making her ugly or less than others. One of the reasons that it is so important that your child knows they can come talk to you is so you can help to alleviate their fears. Reassure your daughter that her body is beautiful, and these changes are natural. Every person's body is different, and that's okay.

Use the glossary to help you discuss female anatomy using their proper terms (vagina, urethra, anus, breasts/nipples, vulva). Doing so can help your daughter feel more comfortable and confident in knowing what her body is going through.

Start the Conversation

Discuss the many parts of the vulva and their functions. If you have a diagram, now is a good time to use it. While you are discussing this subject with your daughter, you might consider encouraging her to look at her vulva in a mirror. It's important for her to know exactly what it looks like and how it works. Don't forget to remind her (during the discussion and after) that every part of her body is special.

 VULVA: *The parts of the female sexual organs that are on the outside of the body.*

Teach your daughter that the anus is near the vagina, but it is completely different and is not typically a sexual organ. And when she urinates, her urine does not come out of her vagina, but out of the urethra, located in front of her vagina. Talk to her about the purpose of breasts and nipples, and that they come in many different shapes, sizes, and colors. None are better than any other; they are just different. Explain the many parts and uses of the vagina. See the glossary for additional definitions.

Questions for your Child

- We've talked about the medically correct terms for these body parts, but there are many slang terms as well. What are some you've heard?
- What are some things that make boys and girls different?
- What are some things that make boys and girls the same?
- Every part of your body is worth protecting. Why do you think yours is worth protecting?
- What questions do you have about your body or how certain body parts work?

Additional Resources:

"Simple Ways to Teach Positive Body Image" from Educate and Empower Kids
"As you work with your child on these skills they will learn how to better understand their bodies and the wonderful things that it does. Developing a positive body image will help them as they enter school and grow to be teenagers."

"The Reasoning for Using Anatomically Correct Terms With Your Kids" from Focus on the Family
This article gives reasons for why it's so important to teach your children correct anatomical terms, one of which is that it lays the foundation for when it's time to talk to your children about sex.

"Three Ways to Teach Our Kids Their Bodies Are Not Just For Looks" from Educate and Empower Kids
"Our bodies are more than just a before-and-after image! We are a beautiful work in progress. As we teach our kids these valuable principles, they too can learn to pay attention to how they feel as they work on their own positive body image without comparing themselves to others."

"How to Teach Kids About Anatomy and the Human Body" from Kids Konnect
This article provides parents with helpful tips on how to get anatomy lessons with your kids to stick in their minds.

4. Puberty for Boys

Kids can sometimes freak out over puberty. For many, it can be a scary thing, going through physical changes that they have no control over. The body they were once comfortable in is now uncomfortable, gawky, and a little bit awkward. In a positive, encouraging manner, discuss with your son the physical changes that he can expect: hair growth in strange places, smelly sweat, voice changes, etc. Also explain that the changes will not only be physical. Emotional changes will come as well, because of increased hormone levels.

Even while your son is asleep, his body will do strange things. Nocturnal emissions ("wet dreams") will come soon enough, as will spontaneous erections ("morning wood").

Start the Conversation

Describe how during puberty, boys begin to grow hair under their arms and in the pubic area. It will grow thickly in areas like the legs and arms and chest. Their sweat glands will produce more, and the area under the arms may smell unpleasant. The nipple and breast area may become tender and swell a bit. Their voice will begin to deepen and may "crack" sometimes due to these changes in the vocal cords. Touch on the emotional sensitivity that may come due to hormonal changes as your son goes through puberty.

NOCTURNAL EMISSIONS: *A spontaneous orgasm that occurs during sleep.*

While you're discussing this with your son and if you feel he is ready, you might want to discuss feelings of arousal and explain that his body's reactions are completely normal and nothing to feel ashamed of. Talk about ways to handle "spontaneous erections" in public situations. Perhaps Dad could share ways that he handles such occurrences, so your son knows has a real example of how he will not be alone in that struggle. Nocturnal emissions or "wet dreams" are a common occurrence at this age and nothing to feel embarrassed about or ashamed of.

Puberty is a great time for kids to learn how to use the washer and dryer because they will have sweaty clothes and sheets. Don't forget to mention that frequent (if not daily!) showering will become a must during this time period. Mention that it helps every guy look and feel better. Be positive! Talk about the amazing things the male body can do.

Questions for Your Child

- Have you noticed any changes in your body?
- Are there any changes in your body that you are looking forward to?
- Is there anything about puberty you're confused or nervous about?
- What's the most exciting thing about growing up?
- Have you noticed other kids your age starting to change?
- How would you feel if you didn't start puberty at the same time your friends did?

Activity

Talk about Dad's experiences with puberty. Discuss his age when he started and how this is sometimes an indicator of when a son will begin. Dad, share your experiences.

Sample Dialogue

Parent: When I was younger, going through puberty, I remember [this] made me very awkward. But I realized that my body is unique and special. By comparing myself to others or believing that having a different body would make me feel better, never left me feeling special but sad. It's when we take pride in the bodies we have that we can gain confidence in ourselves and who we are. Do you ever feel uncomfortable with your body?

(Allow your child to answer.)

Additional Resources:

"Talking With Your Kids About Puberty: You Got This!" from Educate and Empower Kids
"Talking to our kids about puberty can be awkward! But it doesn't have to be! Tackling tough topics with your kids shows them that they can talk to you about cringy subjects without you freaking out."

"Talking to Your Child About Puberty" from Kids Health
This article points out other specific questions that your child may ask, about themselves and others. It gives suggestions on how to approach those questions and what to look out for as your child goes through puberty.

"Alright Dads, No More Sitting On the Side Lines: GET IN THE GAME" from Educate and Empower Kids
"If you are anything like me, you may have separated your responsibilities from your wife's. In the past, our society designated the man as the breadwinner and the woman as the caretaker and housekeeper. We don't live in this world anymore."

"Talking to Your Son About Puberty? Here's How" from Sanford Health
This article gives tips and tricks for during the puberty conversation with your son, and also how to be considerate of what puberty means for a boy.

5. Puberty for Girls

Puberty can be a challenging season as our bodies grow and change so that we can become young women and men. It is the transitional period between childhood and adulthood. Talk openly and positively about these changes that your child is experiencing. Let them know that the changes are normal and that you have gone through them too!

Discuss the physical changes your daughter can expect: hair growth, increased sweat, breast development, menstruation (see the following lesson). Explain that with newly increased hormones, she is likely to experience some emotional changes. Honestly talk about how feelings of arousal, wetness, and discharge in the vaginal area are normal and natural.

Start the Conversation
Describe how even in girls, the body's sweat glands will begin producing more, and any sweat from underneath the arm area could smell unpleasant. They will also begin to grow hair under their arms, in their pubic areas, and experience growth in places like the legs and arms. Breasts will become tender and start to develop. Point out to them that breast development can vary widely in girls and it is usually the signal of the onset of puberty. Discuss how emotional and sensitive girls can become during this time due to the hormonal changes their bodies are going through. When you are discussing with your daughter, and if she is ready, you may want to talk to her about feelings of arousal. Explain that her body's reactions are completely normal and nothing to feel ashamed of. Follow up with the next lesson #6, "Menstrual Cycle."

Puberty is a great time to discuss with your daughter the necessity of purchasing bras and picking out deodorant. You may want to teach her how to shave her legs and under arms as well. Don't forget to mention that frequent (if not daily!) showering will become a must during this time period. Remind her that it helps every girl look and feel better. Be sure to talk about the amazing things the female body can do!

Questions for Your Child
- Have you noticed any changes in your body?
- Are there any changes in your body that you are looking forward to?

- Is there anything about puberty that you're confused about?
- What changes are you nervous about experiencing?
- Growing up can be fun and challenging. How do you picture it?
- Have you talked to any of your friends about these changes? What have you learned?
- What can I do to help you feel more comfortable talking about these changes?

Activity

Mom, tell your daughter about some of your experiences with puberty. If possible, discuss how old you were when you started puberty. Talk about how this is sometimes an indicator of when a daughter will start. Mom, feel free to share the positive and embarrassing parts of your experience.

Additional Resources:

"8 Things Your Daughter Needs to Hear From YOU" from Educate and Empower Kids
Written for mothers to their daughters, this article lists the top eight things that every mother's daughter needs to hear.

"Do Dads Really Matter in the Digital Age?" from Educate and Empower Kids
This webinar with parenting expert, Dr. Tim Rarick, explores the latest research about fathers and the impact that they have on their children, particularly daughters.

"Sex Talks for Daughters" from Parents Aware, featuring Dina Alexander of Educate and Empower Kids
"While we're telling our girls that they can grow up to be anything they want… women are continually portrayed as sex objects on social media and in film and print. Is it surprising then that these scripts find their way into first kisses, dating, and eventual sexual relationships?"

6. Menstrual Cycle

This time is full of differing emotions for a girl. They can be excited to grow up, but also terrified of what is coming their way. Prepare your daughter by calmly and matter-of-factly discussing the facts. Help her understand the physical effects and emotional shifts that occur during a menstrual cycle. Although many girls don't like having a period, remind your daughter of the purpose of it. The menstrual cycle makes it so that women can bear and have children. If you are discussing this with your son, help him to understand that girls may be sensitive or embarrassed by their periods.

Feel free to share with your daughter when your first menstrual cycle started to help her know it is normal and happens to almost all women. You can also prepare her and have her put feminine products in her backpack in case her period starts unexpectedly.

Start the Conversation
Explain to your child that the age of first menstruation is different for everyone, with the average age being 12 years old. Point out that discharge (mucus from vagina) may begin about 6 months before the first period, and continue throughout their life.

If you have a diagram, now may be a good time to use it to explain menstruation. First, the egg is released from the ovaries through the fallopian tube into the uterus. Each month, a lining of blood and tissue build up in the uterus. When the egg is not fertilized, this lining is not needed and is shed from the body through the vagina.

MENSTRUAL PERIOD: *A discharging of blood, secretions, and tissue debris from the uterus as it sheds its thickened lining (endometrium) approximately once per month in females who've reached a fertile age. This does not occur during pregnancy.*

A cycle is roughly 28 days but can vary. Bleeding time lasts from 2-7 days. It may be accompanied by cramping, water retention, breast tenderness, and emotional sensitivity. Point out that there is no way of knowing just by looking at a girl if she is menstruating. Being prepared is a young girl's best bet! Talk about the various methods of containing the period to keep clean, such as sanitary napkins or "pads," tampons (with various kinds of applicators and absorbency levels), and menstrual cups, and explain how each is used. Talk about mood changes that can occur around periods, and how each girl reacts differently to these changing hormone levels.

Questions for Your Child

- What have you heard about menstrual periods?
- How do you feel about getting your period?
- How can a girl be prepared for her period?
- How can people show more sensitivity to a girl during her period?
- Most teenage girls do not like having their period. What can you do so that it doesn't feel like a burden?

Additional Resources:

"Great Mother Daughter Relationships–Set a Tone for Awesomeness" from Educate and Empower Kids
This short article offers mothers support and advice for how they can open the door for those uncomfortable conversations with their daughters.

"Preparing Your Daughter for Her Period: 12 Essential Steps" from Educate and Empower Kids
"Preparing your daughter for her period is an important part of parenting. By providing accurate information, and offering guidance, you can help your daughter approach menstruation with understanding and self-assurance.

"Improve Your Relationship With Your Daughter - Here are Four Ways to Better Communication" from Educate and Empower Kids
"A strong foundation for a father/daughter relationship begins with caring. My dad and I definitely had that going for us, but because the building blocks of a father/daughter relationship roll right into the kind of dating relationships and marriage a girl might have, you need more than just unspoken loyalties."

7. Physical Mechanics of Sexual Intercourse

Take some time to simply and thoroughly discuss the physical mechanics of sex and any additional information your child may need at this developmental stage. Check the glossary for any definitions you may need such as arousal, clitoris, erection, vaginal secretions, oral sex, anal sex, and more.

Allow your child to guide this conversation so you can get an idea of how much information they are ready for. For example, ask your child what they already know about the word "sex" (see Sample Dialogue below). In doing so, you can make sure that you and your child are on the same page and also remind them they are heard. If your child seems ready (perhaps they mention that kids on the playground have been talking about sex or they ask more specific questions), start with the basics. You might wish to speak in the abstract. "A man and a woman each have body parts that fit together…"

Your child will sense if you're uncomfortable, so do your best to relax! Talk about it matter-of-factly, as you would when explaining any topic to your child!

Start the Conversation

Begin by letting your child know that talking about sex can be uncomfortable or awkward for some people, and that is totally okay! Remind them that you are there to answer their questions, even if they feel awkward.

Describe sexual intercourse. Here are the basics: A man places his erect penis into the vagina of his partner. She may help direct him to make insertion easier. One or both partners may thrust rhythmically until the man or both of them orgasm. When he orgasms, sperm is released from his penis.

ORGASM: *The rhythmic muscular contractions in the pelvic region that occur as a result of sexual stimulation during the sexual response cycle. Orgasms are characterized by a sudden release of built-up sexual tension and by the resulting sexual pleasure.*

Typically, a man helps his partner achieve orgasm before focusing on his orgasm. He helps his partner achieve orgasm by stimulating her genitals, especially her clitoris. As she feels more aroused, her vaginal area will become wet with vaginal secretions. This makes the insertion of the penis easier. With proper stimulation, the woman will orgasm. This can happen before the man places his penis into her vagina.

Let your child know that although simultaneous orgasm is often portrayed in media, often one partner orgasms before the other. Discuss how this might be a better way to have intercourse as it allows one person to focus on the pleasure of their partner and then have their partner focus their attention on them.

Sample Dialogue

Parent: I know that a lot of people feel uncomfortable talking about sex. You might feel uncomfortable and that's a normal response for lots of kids and adults. But it's really important that you have correct information. I want you to know that you can always come and ask me questions about sex or anything. So, let's make sure we're on the same page. Can you tell me what you know about the word sex?
(Allow your child to answer.)

> "Our children should be properly introduced to the world in which they live."
>
> —THOMAS BERRY

Questions for Your Child

- Are your classmates talking about sex? How does that make you feel? What do you think about it?
- Why should we not just have sex with anyone? When is it OK to have sex with someone?
- What is something that you should expect to accompany sexual intimacy? (Discuss respect, kindness, and boundaries.)

Additional Resources:

"How to Talk to Kids about Sex" from Dr. Robin Silverman, featuring Dina Alexander of Educate and Empower Kids
This podcast discusses the importance of having a series of little talks with your child, rather than one big one.

"8 Ways to Start Talking to Your Child About Sex" from Educate and Empower Kids
"It can be awkward in the beginning, no doubt, but discussing sexual intimacy is such an important conversation that, as parents, we need to use every healthy way we can to start talking until we find a way that works."

"Common Mistakes Parents Make When Talking to Kids About Sex" from Educate and Empower Kids
This article gives some great advice on how to empower your kids with accurate information.

"Be Your Child's First Choice for Sex Ed - Instead of Google" from Educate and Empower Kids
"Google can be a great resource to help with our jobs, find parenting advice, shop, and may even help prove your friends wrong. On the other hand, Google can contain some extremely harmful content. Imagine how "helpful" it may seem for a curious child."

"'The Talk(s)': Start Off Easy" from Educate and Empower Kids
"It is time to start talking! But we do NOT need to be scared. We have opportunities every single day to talk and connect with our kids, to take time to teach them the difference between online, shallow connections and real-life human intimacy."

8. Emotional Aspects of Sex

Through books, movies, social media, and elsewhere, the popular culture of today tends to portray sex as a purely selfish, physical interaction rather than an action based on a strong relationship. Explain to your child that sex can be a natural expression of emotional love, between people that are committed to and love each other. But sex can also create feelings of confusion and hurt, if it isn't accompanied by love and commitment.

Help your child to understand that sexual acts and emotional intimacy can be two separate things. Sex on its own is usually an empty or selfish experience. It can lower self-esteem, and cause a person to have trouble being emotionally healthy. Better sexual experiences occur in a committed relationship where both partners have real intimacy (mentally and emotionally), mutual respect, and full confidence in the love they share. Discuss the amazing, uniting force that sexual intimacy can be in a relationship.

Start the Conversation

Help your child to understand the connection between emotions and physical expression, like laughing when we think something is funny, stomping a foot when we feel angry, or wanting a hug when we feel sad. Talk about why we only kiss people we like or love. Remind them of the good feelings we get from hugs.

Explain when he or she is ready that these are the same reasons that sex is always better when it's with someone you're committed to. Reiterate the fact that children are not emotionally ready to have sex. Discuss your family's personal values and beliefs about when and with whom it is appropriate to have sex.

Questions for Your Child

- What does "emotional intimacy" feel like? (warmth, happiness, peace, caring, etc.)
- Why does loving someone make people want to express that love in a physical way?
- People often focus on the physical pleasure that sex can bring. What feelings and emotions do you think having sex brings to people?
- Sex often makes us feel bonded and profoundly connected. Why should these feelings be protected?

Additional Resources:

"Intimacy Education Vs Sex Education" from Educate and Empower Kids
This article provides parents with a perspective on how sex education goes beyond the physical aspects of the act and encourages parents to put the topic of sex within the context of relationships and religion as well.

"Beyond the Sex Talks: Teaching Teens Emotional Intimacy" from Educate and Empower Kids
"We want our children to be emotionally healthy, and a large part of that is developing healthy sexuality. …Teaching our kids about the emotional intimacy side of sex is just as important as teaching them about the facts and statistics."

"Helping Your Child Develop Empathy" from Educate and Empower Kids
"Empathy is a critical component in developing emotional intelligence. We develop this skill as we become aware of other people's feelings, needs, and concerns. Empathy is important because it helps us to understand how others are feeling and how our actions might impact them."

"Kids in the Digital Age: The Challenge of Expressing Emotions Healthily" from Educate and Empower Kids
"This new age of digital communication poses new problems… We cannot raise a stronger, more capable generation if we allow them to hide behind their devices rather than educating them in how to properly communicate with one another."

9. Relationships Are Good And Wonderful

Explain to your child that there are many different types of relationships we each experience in our lifetime—friendships, relationships with parents and siblings, romantic relationships, professional relationships, and more. Each of these relationships can be special and wonderful. No relationship is perfect. There are enriching, fun, and difficult aspects of every relationship.

Start the Conversation

Though there aren't any perfect indicators of readiness for a romantic relationship, age, maturity level, personal responsibility, and accountability are a good start. Tell your children experiences that you have learned from over the years that have helped you determine when someone is ready for a relationship.

Discuss the pervasive trend in our culture to have sex with one or multiple partners throughout life without having any committed relationships. Explain your own opinion on this. Talk about the emotional benefits of committed relationships (trust, connectedness) and health benefits (less risk of STIs). This is a great time to talk about how relationships are formed and how they progress over time. You may want to share how you met your child's father/mother (see activity below).

Questions for Your Child

- What is a relationship?
- What is the difference between a sibling relationship and a friendship? What is the difference between a friendship and a romantic relationship?
- Think about your current relationships with your friends and family. Do you treat your family members with the same kindness you treat your friends with?
- What are some ways we can improve our relationships with our friends? Our siblings? Our parents?
- As children, you are learning to get along and be a good friend to others. How will this help you in your future relationships? How will this help you to be a good husband or wife?
- What qualities can a person have that makes being a friend to him or her difficult?
- How can you get out of a relationship or friendship with someone who is unkind or abusive?

Activity
As a family, discuss the most rewarding relationships you have had with friends, relatives, co-workers, or people at school. Allow each person to talk about a friendship they have really valued. This is a great time to talk about how Mom and Dad met. Allow each person to share at least one experience. What made this relationship fun or special? What makes certain relationships just "click"? What can we do to help relationships grow?

Additional Resources:

"15 Things I Want My Son to Know About Love and Sex" from Educate and Empower Kids
"I want my son to experience a unifying, emotionally intimate relationship with the woman he chooses when the time is right for them. Facts and statistics are important, but the humanity of sex is paramount."

"15 Things I Want My Daughter to Know About Love and Sex" by Educate and Empower Kids
"There are conflicting messages about sex everywhere we look: that it's good, that it's bad, that everyone is doing it, that it's important to save it for marriage. There are countless ways pop culture reduces it to unemotional, un-relational entertainment. As a teenage girl navigating her way through the muddle, there are specific things I want my daughter to know about love and sex."

Conversations with My Kids: 30 Essential Family Discussions for the Digital Age from Educate and Empower Kids
An amazing resource full of great family night lessons and discussion questions about relationships, LGBTQ issues, compassion, marriage and divorce and lessons on technology, self-improvement, and so much more!

"Lesson: Kindness: Online, Face to Face, and Everywhere" from Educate and Empower Kids
"Today's culture teaches children that being overly critical of others is a positive thing… Children need parents to help them understand that kindness is not just a quality to have with their friends or family, but at all times."

10. What Does A Healthy Relationship Look Like?

While no relationship is going to be picture-perfect, there are things that are necessary for a relationship to be healthy. Explain that a healthy relationship includes good communication, mutual respect, kindness, and more. Discuss with your child the healthy aspects of some of your friendships and other relationships. Share why you feel comfortable and loved around certain people and what makes you a good friend or parent.

Use the glossary to discuss physical, emotional, and sexual abuse.

Start the Conversation
Help your child to understand that both parties in any relationship are equal. Neither person is above the other and no one, no matter what they have done, deserves to be abused by another person.

Define physical, emotional, and sexual abuse. As you define each of these, allow your child to ask you questions about each of these types of abuse. Share your wisdom and experience. Remind your child that most people are truly good, but that there are bad people in every culture, religion, and neighborhood.

Questions for Your Child
- How do healthy relationships begin?
- What are some unique things you could bring to a dating or marriage relationship?
- What qualities do you look for in a friend?

- What qualities might you look for someday in a significant other?
- Someday when you're dating, how will you know you are in a healthy relationship?
- Do you know what abuse looks like?
- What can you do if someone is abusing you? Who can you get help from?
- What do you think are the differences between a healthy relationship and an abusive one?
- Why is it NOT okay to stay in a relationship where someone hits you even once?
- What adults do you know that have a healthy relationship?
- Why is it important for people in any type of relationship to treat one another with respect?

Sample Dialogue

Parent: Everyone wants and deserves to be loved. And most people want to have a partner that they can share their life with. Someone who they respect and admire, someone they can trust and talk to about anything. What would your ideal person be like? What might they look like? How will you know you have found someone you want to be with forever?

(Allow your child to answer.)

Additional Resources:

"How to Create Healthy Relationships" from Educate and Empower Kids
"Teaching children how to build healthy relationships will enable them to recognize when a relationship is unhealthy, build healthy relationships, and allow them to help others to foster healthy relationships."

"Five Great Ways to Bring Truly Open Communication to Your Home" from Educate and Empower Kids
This article gives 5 suggestions on how to teach yourselves and your children open communication, which will help your children to be able to bring that open communication into whatever relationships they have in the future.

"Real Life Lessons Learned from Beauty and the Beast" from Educate and Empower Kids
"Many portrayals of boys/men in the media allow them a free pass when it comes to their behavior… The audience laughs with a 'boys will be boys' attitude. And what about the male character who doesn't take 'no' for an answer, and the audience views it as romantic?"

"10 Signs of a Healthy Relationship" from Walden University
Psychiatrist George Vaillant, who has led one of the world's longest studies of adult life, has found that "…the key to healthy aging is relationships, relationships, relationships." The current head of the study gives the top 10 indicators of a healthy relationship.

11. Romantic Love

It's essential that our children understand that romantic love is different from physical attraction. Describe how people can be physically attracted to one another without falling in love. Discuss the difference between infatuation and real, long-lasting love.

Make this a fun discussion. Give personal examples from your own life! Talk about how you fell in love with your spouse and/or about the first time you fell in love. Ask your child to share what they think they might want in a future spouse some day.

Start the Conversation

Tell your child that it is normal to love friends and want to spend time together, but that it's different from romantic love. Give examples of how people express romantic love, like kissing, dating, cuddling, etc. Talk about what romantic love means to you, and discuss that romance is something that happens between people who are older, primarily adults. Ask your child what they think they might feel when they are starting to fall in love. Ask them what they think are healthy ways to express that love, so that the person they love can feel and understand how they feel.

Questions for Your Child

- What do you think romantic love is? How is this different from other kinds of love?
- How do people show romantic love? What do you think falling in love feels like?
- People show love in different ways. How do mom and dad show romantic love?
- What other types of affection have you seen?
- How is love portrayed in TV and movies? Do you think they portray love in a realistic way?

 ROMANTIC LOVE: *A form of love that denotes intimacy and a strong desire for emotional connection with another person to whom one is generally also sexually attracted.*

- Q How do you think a married couple should show love to one another?
- Q How will you know you're ready to be in a romantic relationship?

Activity
Watch a family-friendly love story such as *The Sound of Music*, *Sense and Sensibility*, *The Princess Bride*, *Ever After*, *Anne of Avonlea*, or one of your favorites. Throughout the movie or afterward ask your child the following questions:

- Q Do these characters seem like anyone we know in real life?
- Q Is this a realistic depiction of how people fall in love?
- Q Is this how you would like to fall in love?
- Q Do you think their relationship will last?
- Q How do you think you will know you are in love with someone?

Additional Resources:

"Helping Children Develop Healthy Sexual Attitudes" from Educate and Empower Kids
"...it is important to accept the reality that every human being, including your teenager, has an arousal template. Accepting this reality and creating open communication in your home are the key first steps in helping your child develop healthy sexual attitudes."

"Preparing Our Kids for Courtship in the Digital Age" from Educate and Empower Kids
"We live in a NOW society, with little ability to wait for that planned date, wait to be courted, or wait for sex with the right person. This lack of self-restraint has led to an influx of singles–especially teens– experiencing difficulty in understanding how to progress through the phases of courtship."

"The Sex Talk Isn't Enough: How Parents Can Teach Teens About Healthy Relationships" from The Washington Post
"It's not enough to have the sex talk, we have to have the love talk, too. Without it, we risk our kids being in abusive, manipulative relationships, or missing out on a truly wonderful aspect of life."

12. Different Kinds of Families

There are many different kinds of families. Some kids are raised by grandparents, aunts and uncles, or other family members. Some children are raised by a single parent. Some families have two dads or two moms and some kids are raised by one mother and one father. Discuss some of the families you know that are different from yours.

> "Families are like branches on a tree. We grow in different directions, yet our roots remain as one."
> -UNKNOWN

This might be a good time to talk about your family's history. If you have them, show your children pictures of your ancestors. Tell them stories. Teach them about the variety of families they have come from. Feel free to talk about some of the different traditions and behaviors you can decipher from looking deeper into those stories, or delving into your family history (like people marrying their cousins, staying in one town for generations, naming their children in a certain way, etc.).

Start the Conversation

Every family is different and special in its own way. It is important that we love our friends and those we interact with regardless of their family circumstances. Talk with your child about how important family is, and that we should never put down friends for having a different family than ours. There is no such thing as a perfect family. Discuss the different kinds of families you see at church, school, and

in your neighborhood. Make sure to emphasize that everyone has gifts and challenges, and that every family is unique and special. Although families come in different shapes and sizes, they all have value and each family member is a child of God, just like you and your child.

Talk with your child about what simple things they would like to implement when they have their own families. Though no family is perfect, we can all prepare ourselves for what we deem acceptable or not in our families by giving it thought earlier on.

Questions for Your Child

- How would you describe your family?
- Tell me what you imagine your future family will be like? How will that family be similar to your family now? How will it be different?
  - What makes a strong family? What can we do to make our family stronger?
  - How does doing this strengthen our family?
  - Why is it so important for a family to be strong?

Additional Resources:

"Starting Conversations with Your Kids about LGBTQ Identities" from Educate and Empower Kids
"It is important to teach through behavior and conversation that treating others with respect is critical to our communities. This will lead to more tolerance and safety for all people no matter their identity."

"6 Ways to Teach Your Child to Accept Every Type of Family" from Parents
"In a world where all kinds of ties bind parents to their children—whether the grown-ups are single, in a same-sex marriage, or adoptive guardians—it's important to show kids that it's not who's involved, but the love they share that makes a family."

"The Many Kinds of Family Structures in Our Communities" from Sonoma County Office of Education
"One of the most important tasks for early childhood educators is to treat each child's family with respect and help each child feel proud and strong about their family. It is important to learn about the many structures of families and to realize that different families may have quite different issues, needs, strengths and values. The following terms may help you to think carefully and respectfully about each family."

13. Gender & Gender Roles

Throughout history, gender roles have evolved in many different ways. As our culture explores what it means to be a woman and what it means to be a man, it's important to teach our kids how we can elevate the status of women and girls without devaluing men and boys. Teach your kids how in their grandparents' youth, girls had much fewer educational opportunities and were expected to take on most of the responsibility of raising children. Nowadays, parents share the responsibilities of raising children and running a household.

GENDER ROLE: *The pattern of masculine or feminine behavior of an individual that is defined by a particular culture and that is largely determined by a child's upbringing.*

At school, work, and within our families, we sometimes let stereotypical gender roles stop us from trying something new or speaking up on certain topics.

Discuss the division of indoor and outdoor chores for your home and your thoughts on the various roles and responsibilities of men and women. Talk about the strengths of various men and women you know.

Start the Conversation

Encourage a good conversation about stereotyping and typical male and female roles. Remind your kids that although our bodies and physical abilities are different in fundamental ways, women and men can perform mental and emotional tasks equally well. Share your personal thoughts.

Ask: How do both of your parents contribute to your home and family? Both boys and girls are necessary in our families, wards, and communities. What are some ways you would like to contribute to your family and community?

Explain to your child how the fetus actually becomes male or female. Soon after conception, all children have internal and external sex organs in a simple form. This differentiation between the two genders—male and female—

progresses throughout physiological development until there are complete internal and external female or male reproductive organs. The reproductive organs that develop while in the womb for the male fetus include testes, penis, and the scrotum. The female fetus develops two ovaries (which contain all the egg cells she will have during a lifetime), the uterus (womb), the vagina, and labia. At birth the male or the female infant has reproductive organs but lacks reproductive capacity. This comes at puberty.

Help your child understand that the world's ideas about gender, gender expression, and gender identity are changing rapidly! But the most important thing for them to remember is that they always need to be okay with themselves. They're the person living their life; they know who they are better than anyone.

Questions for Your Child

- Are there typical boy and girl interests?
- Is it okay for boys and girls to pursue whatever activities they are interested in doing?
- Is it okay for boys to be interested in what are thought of as feminine things and for girls to be interested in typically masculine things?
- Why is it important to look past a friend's likes or outward appearance, and instead focus on who they really are?

Additional Resources:

"Ways to Empower Children Regardless of Gender" from Educate and Empower Kids
"By teaching our children to value all people, we must be prepared to judge less, respect more and advocate for a world where all humans, regardless of gender, are allowed to reach their full potential."

"Understanding Gender Identity Terminology: A Guide for Parents" from Educate and Empower Kids
"Whether you agree with the idea of choosing one's gender or not, it is helpful for every parent to keep up with the concerns, trends, and shifts in societal norms and language."

"Gender and Health" from WHO
"This Q&A examines the links between gender and health, highlighting WHO's ongoing work to address gender-related barriers to healthcare, advance gender equality and the empowerment of women and girls in all their diversity, and achieve health for all."

14. Sexual Identification

This is a great opportunity to teach your kids about the various kinds of sexual identifications. Your child has probably already heard something of one or more of them. Define each one and be ready to answer your child's questions.

Use the glossary to help you discuss heterosexual, gay, lesbian, bisexual, transgender, asexual, and intersex identifications.

Start the Conversation

First, explain the difference between friend love and sexual attraction. Make it clear that liking someone or being a fan of someone who is gay (a friend or on TV) does not make someone gay. You can even love your friends without being "in love" with them.

With so much hypersexualized media and pornography available to kids, media can sometimes influence how a child or teen sees themselves sexually. Sometimes friends' sexual identity or pressuring parents can influence one's sexual identity. Teach your child that no one's sexuality should be influenced by anyone or anything else. Ask your child what his or her thoughts are on the subject.

Describe how identifying oneself as any particular sexuality does not strictly define a person. One's sexuality is an integral part of them but it does not define who they are. No matter what happens in their life, they will always be your child, and you will always love and accept them.

Note: *Reiterate that we should never mistreat people for being different or having a different sexual identity as you! Share your personal thoughts and understanding of the topic.*

SEXUAL IDENTIFICATION: *How one thinks of oneself in terms of whom one is romantically or sexually attracted to.*

Questions for Your Child

- How do you like to be treated? How do you treat those who are gay, lesbian, or straight?
- What do your classmates and teachers say about homosexuality?
- What should you do if you experience feelings of same sex attraction? Who is a trusted loved one that you can talk to about this?
- What does LGBTQI stand for?
- What does it mean to be gay?
- How are gay people and straight people different?
- How are those who identify as gay (or any of the other terms listed above) not different from others at all?

> "Empathy is choosing to see ourselves in another despite our differences. It's recognizing that the same humanity - the same desire for meaning, fulfillment and security - exists in each of us, even if it's expressed uniquely."
>
> -Vivek Murthy

Additional Resources:

"Guess Who's Coming to Dinner Now" from Educate and Empower Kids
"As parents, it's important to know that the experts agree that no matter your child's sexual orientation the best thing you can do is to let that child know they are loved."

"LGBT Youth Resources" from the CDC
"On this page, find resources from the CDC, other government agencies, and community organizations for LGBT Youth, their friends, educators, parents, and family members to support positive environments."

"Parents: Use the Power of Response Questions" from Educate and Empower Kids
This article provides helpful tips for parents on how to use response questions: what they are and why they are important, as well as the benefits that they can bring to your relationship with your children.

15. At What Age Is Someone Ready For A Sexual Relationship?

Discuss with your child the various stages of a physical relationship: handholding, hugging, kissing, petting, and sexual intercourse. Explain that people are ready for these stages at different ages, but that there are reasons why it might be better to not seriously date or engage in these activities until after the age of 16. Talk about these reasons. Point out that teenagers are not emotionally ready for sexual relationships, and that children are neither physically nor emotionally ready either.

Remind your children that sexual intimacy, curiosity, and sexual desires are all natural feelings, and that they are good. But it can be hurtful to their emotional and mental health to do these things before they are ready.

Start the Conversation
Teach the natural physical progression of a HEALTHY sexual relationship. Explain that a healthy sexual relationship is one in which both parties feel equally respected. Talk about how most healthy marriages start off as friendships and begin with smaller acts

of intimacy (kissing, hugging, cuddling) before moving on to more intimate acts like sexual intercourse.

Discuss the aspects that show one is ready for dating, marriage, and sex. These may include: age, maturity level, capabilities, and personal responsibility. Reiterate your personal or family standards on this subject.

Questions for Your Child

- Q What factors should be considered to determine if someone is ready for sex?
- Q Many teenagers are having sex at younger and younger ages. Why do you think that is?
- Q What age do you think it is okay to start having sex? Is there a right age for everyone?
- Q What are the benefits of waiting to have sex until you are married?
- Q Someday you will be dating. What can you do if someone is pressuring you to have sex and you do not want to?

Additional Resources:

"From Awkward to Awesome: Talking To Your Kids About Sexual Intimacy" from Educate and Empower Kids
This video gives tips and tricks on how to address this topic with your children, and what you can do to make it easier and more beneficial for both you and your child.

"Sex Ed Isn't Just for Kids" from Educate and Empower Kids
"If you're not sure you've mastered the subject of sex, you are not alone. If your own discomfort, disappointment or sexual demons* interfere with your communications with your kids, it is time to do something about it."

"Is the Media Teaching Your Kids Sex?" from Educate and Empower Kids
In this age of media, can you really be sure that filters you have in place are keeping sensitive topics from your child? Make sure they hear them from you, not the screen!

16. Curiosity

Teach your child that curiosity about sex, your developing body, and other's bodies is normal and natural. Being curious is what has kept our species evolving and improving since we first appeared on Earth. Your children are going to have questions about sex. Being a good source for them to come to and ask those questions is essential for their understanding and decision making.

Emphasize to your kids that they should never feel ashamed for being curious, and let them know they can talk to you anytime they feel curious about anything they might have questions about. Explain why parents are the best source of information and how friends at school often have wrong or only partially correct information. You will find more helpful information regarding curiosity when you teach lesson #23, "Pornography."

Start the Conversation
It's so important that children never be made to feel embarrassed for being curious. It's completely natural! Validate your child's awareness and answer questions honestly and completely.

Make them feel as comfortable as possible when they come to you with questions. Remind them that your home is a safe zone where questions are always okay. If some topics are too awkward to ask questions about face to face, give your kids the option to write it down.

Questions for Your Child

- Why is curiosity a good thing?
- Who should you talk to if you are curious about your body? About sex? About members of the opposite gender?
- How is curiosity essential to learning?
- What are some things about your body that you are curious about?
- What else are you curious about?
- Would you like to know more about (pick your own topic) …?
- What can I do to help you feel more comfortable coming to me with questions?

Activity

Share an experience with your child about a time you were curious about something.

- How did you find more information?
- Was this a good experience or not?
- Did your parents have any particular reaction to your curiosity?
- Were you able to ask your parents awkward questions?

> "Curiosity is the wick in the candle of learning."
> –William Arthur Ward

Additional Resources:

7 Steps to Take to Establish Yourself as an Approachable Parent" from Educate and Empower Kids
"…the advice I am most comfortable doling out, is to prioritize becoming an approachable parent. In other words, you want to learn how to listen to your kids talk about sex, not just learn what to say to them about sex."

"Teaching Without Shame: Understanding Your Child's Curiosity" from Educate and Empower Kids
This article tells the story of a mother talking through her son's curiosity with him and helping him understand that our bodies are beautiful and natural, but that we each deserve our own privacy as well.

"Sexual Curiosity: A (Happy) Postcard from a Dad in the Trenches" from Educate and Empower Kids
"We talked about useful ways to respond to sexual curiosity and arousal. We talked about acknowledging those feelings, experiencing gratitude for them, and then how he could put them in their place within the wider context of his life, his values, and his goals. We talked about how sexual curiosity and arousal can powerfully bond loving couples."

17. Masturbation

Everyone has different opinions when it comes to masturbation. Even though (medically) the behavior can be a normal part of a child's development, for some, there are other reasons parents may wish to discourage masturbation. Explain your personal views with your child about masturbation. Talk about the necessity of privacy, appropriate times, places, etc. Discuss the possibility of addiction. However you choose to talk about masturbation with your child, it is important to let them know that they are loved. Remind your child about the impulses kids start feeling around puberty and how normal and natural those feelings are. Point out healthy ways they can handle those impulses. Make sure to tell your child why you believe the way that you do.

Some say that masturbation is an unnecessary, self-interested behavior and worry that it can teach a child to indulge in impulsive behavior and may take away from the "giving" aspect of future sexual experiences. If you believe that masturbation is healthy or unhealthy, tell your child and explain WHY.

Since masturbation often accompanies pornography viewing, you may wish to discuss this lesson in conjunction with lesson #23, "Pornography." Please also keep in mind that many young children explore their genitals or masturbate for the simple reason that it feels good. They may not even be trying to achieve orgasm. This discussion is different, and is for an older child that understands the "purpose" of masturbation.

MASTURBATION: *Self-stimulation of the genitals in order to produce sexual arousal, pleasure, and/or orgasm.*

Start the Conversation

Explain that masturbation is self-stimulation of the genitals and that most people do it to achieve orgasm. Discuss your personal views with your child about masturbation. Discuss privacy and appropriate times, places, etc. Discuss the possibility of addiction, especially if a child begins masturbating often at a young age. Explain that it can sometimes be a habit-forming behavior. Discuss the pros and cons of forming various habits. Talk about the impulses kids start feeling around puberty and how normal and natural those feelings are. Talk about healthy ways they can handle those impulses.

Discuss coping mechanisms and how many people use masturbation to cope with stress, loneliness, boredom, etc. Explain that everyone uses coping mechanisms. Talk about various options for coping with life experiences.

"Shame is that warm feeling that washes over us, making us feel small, flawed, and never good enough."

—BRENÉ BROWN

However you choose to talk about masturbation with your child, it is important to avoid shaming your child. Let them know that they are loved no matter what. Remember, some kids are simply using masturbation to explore their bodies or to relax.

Questions for Your Child

- Do you understand what masturbation is?
- Is it healthy to explore our bodies? What is the difference between exploring and masturbating?
- Is masturbation good? Bad? Neither? If you masturbate, are you a bad person? (No!)
- What is an appropriate time and place for masturbation?
- Is it okay to masturbate once a week? Once a month? Once a day?
- What other activities or coping mechanisms could you do in place of masturbation (read a book, go on a walk, play a game, talk to a friend, draw, bake, etc.)?
- Are there consequences if masturbation becomes a habit?
- If this or any other habit in your life becomes an issue for you, who can you talk to about it?
- Many people often feel ashamed of masturbating, so they hide what they are doing from their parents. Why is hiding behavior from our parents unhealthy?

Additional Resources:

"Talking with Our Kids about Masturbation—Without Shame!" from Educate and Empower Kids
This article helps offer parents a variety of ways that they can choose to approach discussing masturbation.

"Talking with Our Daughters about Masturbation" from Educate and Empower Kids
This article discusses how parents can approach their daughters specifically about the topic of masturbation.

"What Are You Most Scared About Teaching Your Young Children?" from Educate and Empower Kids
Talking to your kids shouldn't be scary, no matter what it is you're talking about. This video can help you to relieve the pressure you feel!

18. Children DO NOT Have Sex

It may seem like common sense that children do not have sex. However, as kids are exposed to pornography, hypersexualized media, and spend large amounts of time online, something as basic as this needs to be taught!

As a family, create a plan of what your kids can do if someone touches them inappropriately, tries to show them pornography, tries to be alone with them, or any other situation that you think your children should be prepared for. This and the following lessons have several teaching points to guide you.

Start the Conversation
Explain to your child that an adult you can trust will never say it is normal for a child to have sex. Children's bodies are not physically mature or ready for sex. Children also have a different emotional capability than adults. These are reasons why children DO NOT have sex. Share these reasons with your child. Remind your child that sex is for grown-ups. Not kids. It is against the law for someone to have sex with a child. Teach your kids you ALWAYS have the right to say "NO!"

> "There is no trust more sacred than the one the world holds with children. There is no duty more important than ensuring that their rights are respected, that their welfare is protected, that their lives are free from fear and want and that they can grow up in peace."
>
> –Kofi Annan

Questions for Your Child
- Has anyone ever touched you in a place that is covered by your bathing suit?
- Has anyone told you to take off your clothes except for mom and dad?

- Q What can you do if someone tries to touch you in a place that is covered by your bathing suit?
- Q Ninety percent of sexual abuse is perpetrated by people we know (a friend, step-sibling, a coach, uncle, etc.). Who are the few people that we trust with absolute certainty? (This should be a very small list of 2-5 people that your kids can rely on with 100% confidence.)
- Q What should you do if someone tells you that sex is normal for children? Why do you think someone would say that?
- Q What should you do if someone asks you to have sex or tries to touch the private parts of your body? Has this ever happened to you?
- Q What should you do if a friend tells you they are being sexually abused by someone? Who can you talk to?

Additional Resources:

"My Body is Mine: Teaching Kids Appropriate Touch" from Educate and Empower Kids
"Teaching your children about appropriate touch will empower them to stand up for themselves and their bodies."

"Teaching Consent. Starting Early and Simply." from Educate and Empower Kids
"[W]e can start teaching our children about consent at a young age by teaching respect for others and boundaries, which are all vital components of a child's developing healthy sexuality."

"Three Generations of Silence: How Do We Turn This Around?" from Educate and Empower Kids
This article discusses how sexual assault/harassment is something that is often brushed under the rug. It offers a variety of ways that mothers can help ensure that their daughters know when to speak up.

"Is Your 12 Year Old HOT Enough? She Better Not Be!" from Educate and Empower Kids
There are simple things you can do every day to help your child know where their true worth lies-within themselves.

19. What To Do If Something Has Happened to You - Who To Talk To

Teach your child that if something happens to them that makes them feel uncomfortable or hurts them, they can ALWAYS tell you, that you are on their side, and that you love them no matter what. Be specific in defining what it means to feel uncomfortable—feeling or causing discomfort or unease; disquieting. Give your child examples of times that you felt uncomfortable or bring up a time you observed that your child was uncomfortable.

> "If children feel safe, they can take risks, ask questions, make mistakes, learn to trust, share their feelings, and grow."
>
> -Alfie Kohn

Remind your child that they should always tell someone right away if they are ever touched in a way that makes him or her feel uncomfortable. Discuss who some trustworthy adults are in your family's life. These can include doctors, police officers, and parents. However, teach your child that no one should make anyone feel uncomfortable, not even trusted adults.

Start the Conversation

Make sure your child understands that if they report that someone has touched them inappropriately, they are NOT in trouble. Explain why it is important to tell a trusted adult. It's important to look for physical cues here. Inform your child that it's important to tell right away, but also that it's never too late. Give reassurance that he or she will be believed. Talk about the adults in your child's life who you trust. Ask your child to list a few people who they trust. Confirm or correct the people on this list. Remind your child that sometimes kids touch or abuse other kids. Discuss with your child what can be done in these circumstances.

Questions for Your Child

- Other than getting a spanking from a parent, have you ever been hurt by a grown up or older child before? ("Hurt" can mean hitting, slapping, screaming, calling someone terrible names, touching someone on their private parts, etc.)
- Has any adult ever told you not to tell Mom or Dad something?
- Why is it a poor choice to keep secrets from your parents?
- Has anyone ever touched you, talked to you, or shown you something sexual that made you feel uncomfortable?
- What would you do if this happened to you?
- Who are adults we can trust? Is there anyone who makes you uncomfortable?

Activity

Talk about what to do if your child reports inappropriate behavior to an adult, only to have it be brushed aside. Discuss options in this scenario like finding another adult or calling someone on their trusted adults list.

Additional Resources:

"How to Make Your Home a Safe Space" from Educate and Empower Kids
"...it can sometimes be tough to create a safe and fun space when new technology often presents many different kinds of dangers. These can very quickly take away from the safe space you're trying to create. But there are plenty of simple, meaningful things we can do to create a warm, inviting safe space for our families and friends."

"Helping Your Child Become the Master of Their Body: Moving Beyond Good Touch/Bad Touch" from Educate and Empower Kids
This family night lesson will guide you in how to help your kids feel comfortable and in control of their bodies, danger signs to look for from predators, how to help your child say "no" to unwanted affection, and more.

"Vigilant Parenting in the Digital Age" from Educate and Empower Kids
"Simply telling our children how to act on the internet is just not enough. We need to be aware of the dangers around, as well as be vigilant in monitoring technology use in our homes… We also must have many discussions with our children about technology use."

20. How Predators Groom Children

This can be a tough lesson to discuss with your kids, but it may be one of the most important lessons you ever teach. We highly recommend reading our short article "8 Ways a Predator Might Groom Your Child" as you prepare.

Help your child understand what it means for someone to groom a child or teenager. Be real and honest! Discuss common grooming techniques with your child. Define what it means to be a predator—a sexual predator is someone who seeks to obtain sexual contact through pursuing, grooming, and/or hunting.

Be frank with your child. Let them know that predators are often people the child knows. Teach them what it means to listen to your instincts. Remind your children that they should never keep secrets about sex from parents.

Start the Conversation

Explain to your kids that predators may seek to gain the victim's trust, then start to desensitize the child to physical touch by using innocent, affectionate touch, such as a pat on the back or a squeeze of an arm. Predators can sometimes be "friends" or peers. They will seek to isolate their victims and/or seek to fill a void in the child's life. Remind your child that no one has a right to touch him or her without his or her consent, not even relatives or grown-up friends.

Talk specifically about your family's policies for taking rides, texting, private messaging, spending time alone with adults and teens who are not on the "trusted adults list." This is also a good time to talk about online predators who might contact your kids through gaming sites, social media, etc. Emphasize the need to be honest with you about their online behavior and to never speak to strangers online—even if they seem to be other kids.

 GROOM: *To prepare or train someone for a particular purpose or activity. In the case of sexual predators, it is any willful action made by the offender to prepare the victim and/or the victim's support network that allows for easier sex offending.*

Finally, you must teach your child that if a peer or adult hurts or abuses them, it is not your child's fault. It is the fault of the perpetrator.

Questions for Your Child

- Do predators look a certain way? Are they always adults? Do they look ugly and mean, or do they look like everyone else?
- When a predator is trying to get you to do something, how might he or she act? Kind? Charming? Friendly?
- Is it possible for a predator to be in your community? Like at church or school?
- It's rare for a stranger to try to take a child from a park, mall, or elsewhere. But why should we never get into cars or go anywhere with strangers?
- What are some warning signs we can look for in adults or teens? (progressive, inappropriate touch, privately texting your child, etc.)
- What are some ways we can stay safe from online predators?

Activity
Present the following scenario to your child:

> You just joined the community soccer team and you're really excited! When you started out, it was nothing but fun, but soon you started to feel uneasy because of the attention of your coach. He never seems to pay as much attention to the other players as he does to you. He brings you small treats or gifts, and he always seems to find a reason to put his hand on your shoulder at every practice. At first you were flattered, but now it's making you uncomfortable and you're not sure why or what to do.

Ask the following questions:
- What would you do in this situation?
- Who should you talk to first?
- Is it okay to say "no" if something makes you uncomfortable? (YES! You can always say "NO!")

Additional Resources:

"A Lesson for Teaching Your Children About Predators" from Educate and Empower Kids
A simple family night lesson to help parents teach their children about predators.

"What Online Predators Don't Want YOU to Do" from Educate and Empower Kids
This article provides a few tips on what you can do to prevent a predator's access to your kids.

"Child Predators: What Every Parent Should Know" from Educate and Empower Kids
Unfortunately, oftentimes it's families and friends who pose a threat to our children. Learn what to look out for to protect your child against whoever may be threatening them.

21. How To Say "NO!"

Saying "no" to an adult can be very difficult for a child. How often were you comfortable saying "no" to an adult when you were a child? It is essential that you practice and give your kids scenarios where it is okay, and even smart, to say "no."

Explain when you expect your children to be obedient—for example, when asked to clean a room or do the dishes. But make it clear to them that there are times when they'll need to have the courage to say "NO!" to an adult.

Sometimes a child may engage in something inappropriate without realizing its repercussions. They may play a game of "show me yours and I'll show you mine" not fully realizing until later that this is a poor choice. Explain that even if they have done something in the past, it doesn't mean they have to do it again.

Start the Conversation
Discuss different types of dangerous situations your child may encounter, such as when he or she is made to feel uncomfortable by what someone does or says. Talk about which situations your child can say no in, not just who they can say "no" to. Examples may include: a friend daring them to pull their pants down, an older cousin who wants to be alone with them in a bedroom, a schoolmate encouraging them to join in teasing someone, a coach who stays in the locker room while their team changes their clothes, etc.

Teach your child that they have the power to say "no" to anyone, including teachers, church leaders, coaches, aunts, grandparents, and whoever else may be in your child's life. Practice saying "no" loudly and firmly. Then practice yelling "NO!"

Questions for Your Child

- Saying "no" to a grown up like a coach or a friend's parent can be very difficult. What can we do to be brave enough to do this?
- What are some instances where we should say "no"? (When someone tries to share drugs or alcohol with us, tries to show us pornography, when an adult tries to get us to be alone with them, when an older child tries to touch us innappropriately, etc.)
- Have you ever had to tell a friend, loved one, or an adult "no"?
- What can you say or do if someone tries to touch you on the private areas of your body, tries to take your clothes off, or tries to take your picture when you are wearing a bathing suit or less clothes? (Yell NO! and run to a safe adult.)
- What are some other circumstances where you can say "No"?

Activity

Create a plan with your child. Ask them what they can do if they are at a friend's house and an older kid or adult makes them feel uncomfortable, tries to get them alone, etc.

- Can they call you and say a "safe word" that your family has agreed on? What else can your child do?
- What are some other circumstances where they may need to use a "safe word"?

Additional Resources:

"Kids and 'Affection': Why I'm NOT Teaching My Kids To Be Polite" from Educate and Empower Kids
This article outlines the importance of helping kids say "no" to unwanted affection and letting them know that they will be believed if something does happen.

"Can You Spot the Grooming Behaviors of a Predator?" from Educate and Empower Kids
This lesson teaches a few tactics on how to recognize grooming behaviors and has multiple links to more helpful resources.

"How to Identify A Child Predator Online" from Educate and Empower Kids
As pedophilia becomes increasingly normalized online, parents need to pay special attention to terms and various code words being used on social media and elsewhere. This helpful guide identifies terms, code words, and symbols used by child predators online.

22. Your Instincts Keep You Safe

Instincts are an amazing part of our body's protection system; the autonomic nervous system that works with the endocrine system to prepare the body for fight or flight.

Teach your child that they have instincts to help them, keep them safe, and can even help them make good decisions. Even if your child hasn't consciously noticed something or someone that could be a threat, the subconscious (their body) may have picked up on it, and is trying to protect them.

Parents, it is crucial that you remind your kids of some of the teachings in lesson #20, "How Predators Groom Children." You must explain that even if one's instincts (gut feelings) prompt you to get out of a situation and you don't, if an adult or peer hurts or abuses them in any way, it is still NOT your child's fault. It is the fault of the perpetrator.

Start the Conversation

To begin discussing instincts, describe a scenario for your child like seeing a big spider or snake or someone jumping out to scare you. Ask your child if they have ever had "gut" or instinctual feelings, either positive or negative. This may feel like an "icky" feeling or feeling "off". Ask your child what that "icky" feeling is trying to tell them. Discuss how this "icky" feeling might occur to their body: pounding heart, stomach ache, a clenching of the heart or or chest, etc. Talk about how we can be more sensitive to these feelings in various situations.

 INSTINCT: *An inherent inclination towards a particular behavior. Behavior that is performed without being based on prior experience is instinctive.*

Explain that instincts are similar to an alarm system that we can feel in a dangerous or uncomfortable situation. Teach your child that it is very important they trust their instincts and listen to their body. Whether it is a certain situation with other kids or a certain person that gives them an "icky" feeling, they need to act on that instinct and do their best to get out of the situation. Explain that they cannot ignore them just because they don't want to make the other person feel bad. Their safety is more important!

Questions for Your Child

- Why are instincts important?
- Instincts feel different to different people. What do instincts feel like to you?
- Do you think you've ever felt your instincts before?
- What are some times or places that our instincts may try to warn us?
- What should you do if you are second-guessing your instincts?
- Who can you talk to if someone or a certain situation gives you that "icky" feeling?

Activity
Mom or Dad, share a story from your life about when you felt like you needed to do or NOT do something. Was it a feeling in your gut? What did it feel like? Did you just suddenly move or act a certain way without fully knowing why? Maybe it was a thought in your mind that wouldn't go away. Did you listen or not? What was the consequence of that action?

> "Instinct is a marvelous thing. It can neither be explained nor ignored."
>
> -Agatha Christie

Additional Resources:

"The Secret I Almost Did Not Tell" from Educate and Empower Kid
In this article, the author shares her own experience with sexual assault as a child and what parents can do to help stop it.

"Protecting Special Needs Children from Unwanted Sexual Attention" from Educate and Empower Kid
"According to research on vera.org, special needs children are 2.9 times more likely to be sexually abused and 4.6 times more likely if that disability is mental or intellectual."

"Sexual Assault Awareness - Conversation Starters to Protect Your Children" from Educate and Empower Kid
Establish yourself as someone your child can trust, and make sure they're comfortable talking to you about these things!

23. Pornography

Pornography (porn) is where our children and teens are learning some of the most repugnant, unhealthy messages about sex, love, relationships, and body image. It is damaging to individuals, relationships, and society. This is such an important lesson! Please take plenty of time to discuss this lesson and don't be afraid to repeat it.

Develop a plan for what to do if your child is exposed to pornography. Use our RUN Plan, found at educateempowerkids.org, to create a plan for the next time your child is exposed to pornography. Here is a summary:

Recognize what you've seen and get away from it

Understand what you've seen and talk about how it made you feel with a trusted adult

Never seek it out again

For more detailed help, check out our book, *How to Talk to Your Kids About Pornography*.

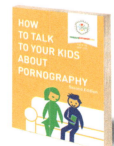

Start the Conversation

Define pornography with the following help. Pornography is pictures or videos of people with little or no clothing. Usually there is sexual behavior in it, but it is always objectification, and it is made for the sole purpose of making money. Help your child understand that objectification is turning a person into a mere thing or object, and choosing to see them without feelings or intelligence.

Explain that it is sometimes used to aid in the sexual abuse of children. Clarify that it is not romantic or at all about love. Describe how it can be addictive. Formulate a plan for what to do if your child sees pornography. Teach them to get away from it, find a trusted adult, and tell a parent. The majority of pornography is now viewed on smart phones and tablets; prepare your child for this probability.

Ask your child if he or she has ever seen pornography. Share your personal or family standards about pornography. Explain that there is nothing wrong with being curious about the human body, that it is natural. But pornography is not a healthy way to find answers about the body or sex.

Questions for Your Child

- Have you ever seen pornography? Where did you see it? What else can you tell me?
- Where are some places you might see porn? (While doing homework, on the school bus, at a friend's house, etc.)
- It's good to be curious, but why is looking at pornography to satisfy your curiosity wrong?
- At some point, you will see pornography. What should you do? Who can you tell?
- Will you make a choice and a commitment right now to never seek out pornography?
- What steps can you take to ensure you stick to this commitment?

Activity
Role play various scenarios where your child is "exposed" to pornography. Model what they can say to a friend or family member who shows them. Discuss what they should do if it pops up on a home or school computer. Have your child take a turn (or several) acting out what they can do if exposed at school, at practice, at church, at a friend's house, etc. Talk about how good kids, who are good friends may be the ones to show your child porn. Act out how your child can get away from seeing pornography and who they can talk to about it.

Additional Resources:

"So You've Had Your First "P*orn Talk." Now What? from Educate and Empower Kids
This video is a clip from UCAP (Utah Coalition Against Pornography) 2016. It introduces research and the effects of pornography and children, and how to talk to your kids about it.

"Porn Addiction is Not Just a Boys' Problem Anymore." from Educate and Empower Kids
Even the idea that your daughter may have a problem with porn can be shocking; having a plan can help you to be calm as you address this topic with your children.

"Dads Kill Porn" from Educate and Empower Kids
"[A] dad's warmth and consistent presence appear to have a protective impact on his daughter's sexual development and activity. Conversely, a fatherless daughter may experience sexual development that can far outpace her emotional, social, and neurological development."

24.
Sexting & Social Media

The research is pouring in, smartphones and social media contribute to depression, anxiety, suicidal ideation, and other mental illnesses in teenagers. Please consider giving your child or teen a phone that does not have internet access (there are several brands now).

Before giving your child a smartphone ask yourself:

- How will my child owning a smartphone contribute to our family's health and happiness?
- How will owning a smartphone help my child to be a kinder, more successful person?
- Does my child really need a phone at school to be successful? (Ask your child's teachers. 90-100% of them will say "no.")

Whether your child has a phone or not, they need to understand the powerful messages in social media and the serious consequences of sexting. Consider downloading our free ebook *Social Media and Teens : The Ultimate Guide to Keeping Kids Safe Online* and discussing its content and discussion questions together as a family.

Explain to your child that any sexually explicit image or video of a child or teenager is considered child pornography (child abuse sexual material) and that your child can get into serious trouble with school administration and law enforcement for having these.

 SEXTING: *The sending or distribution of sexually explicit images, messages, or other material via mobile phones.*

Start the Conversation
Go over your household rules for cell phone and social media use. Discuss why these rules benefit everyone and help keep you safe. Consider installing filters and blocks on your computer and child's phone if you have not yet done so. Explain to your children that

many kids' first porn exposure happens through social media. Teenagers really should not get any sort of social media account until they are at the very least 13, but hopefully won't be allowed on until they are older.

Explain to your child what a sexually explicit text (or sext) is. Discuss what they should do if someone sends them an inappropriate message or sext message. Come up with a plan.

Questions for Your Child

- Social media can be a great tool for people to share uplifting quotes and thoughts. Why do most kids and adults have such a hard time using this technology for good?
- Why do so many kids and adults spend hours on social media each day?
- Can a person really feel good about themselves after spending an hour or two looking at other people's curated photos and posts?
- Who can you talk to if someone asks you for nude photos?
- What can you do if someone asks you for a nude photo or picture of your breasts or other parts of your body?
- Why is it rude or even sexual harassment to ask someone for a sexually explicit photo?
- Why is it unwise to send a naked picture of yourself?

Additional Resources:

Noah's New Phone: A Story about Using Technology for Good from Educate and Empower Kids
A great family night book featuring a poignant story that addresses smartphone rules, online bullying, social media, and more.

"Teaching Social Media Literacy" from Educate and Empower Kids
This family night lesson can "help your children to understand that the edited photos and exciting lives shown on social media are not an accurate portrayal of their everyday life."

"Parents, Do You Know the Most Common Emojis Used in Sexting?" from Educate and Empower Kids
Sometimes it can feel like your child is texting using hieroglyphics, and you have no idea what they're saying. This article breaks it down, and points out some emojis that can be a problem.

25. Being Media Savvy

Media; we are surrounded by it and heavily influenced by it. For the developing brain of a child, media can profoundly influence how they think of themselves, their bodies, sex, gender, marriage, religion, money, and many other things. Explain to your child how media (TV, movies, pop music, social media, etc.) sends us many unhealthy messages about sex, people, love, and relationships. They must learn to think carefully when choosing media and internalizing its messages.

Teaching our kids to be media literate will not only help them to see through the false and unhealthy messages they are exposed to, it will help them understand the world around them in a whole new way. Discuss with them the techniques used in video games, online videos, commercials, billboards, etc. to create "perfect" looking people, representing a very narrow definition of beauty.

Consider reading our book, *Petra's Power to See: A Media Literacy Adventure*. Your child will learn about media, how to understand its messaging, and how to choose media wisely.

Start the Conversation

Teach your children to question the messages they see in all forms of media, especially messages about sex and love. Ask your kids if they have ever had a negative thought about their body after watching a commercial or video. Discuss ways to counteract the

HYPER-SEXUALIZED: *To make overly sexual; to accentuate the sexuality of. Often seen in media.*

false messages they see every day such as using positive self-talk, knowing the truth about media images, etc. Talk about the fact that commercials are all trying to sell a product and that we should always be looking for the underlying message.

Questions for Your Child

- What are some TV shows or movies that have healthy, positive messages? What are some shows or YouTube videos that don't have healthy messages?

- What are some of the messages we see in TV or movies about love, sex, or relationships? Are these healthy or helpful messages?

- Why is there so much sexual content and violence in certain shows and movies?

- What are some of the messages our friends share on social media?

- How much time should a person spend on a phone or staring at a screen each day?

- What happens to our mood and overall mental health when we are on screens too much?

Activity

Deconstructing Media: Watch a commercial with your child and encourage him or her to deconstruct the images and messages within it. Ask your child the following questions:

- What are your first impressions of this commercial? How did it make you feel?

- Why was this advertisement made? What was it trying to sell?

- What values were expressed? What values were not present?

- Did the actors look like people in our neighborhood?

- Were the images in the commercial hyper-sexualized or hyper-masculine?

- After considering the ad this way, how does it make you look at commercials differently?

Additional Resources:

"A Family's Guide to Digital Media" from Educate and Empower Kid
This free e-book was created to assist you and your family in finding a media balance by providing you the tools and information you need to create your own family media usage plan.

"A Lesson About Media Literacy" from Educate and Empower Kid
"Encourage your child to think about not only the images they see, but the messages that are being presented in the images they see–this is teaching them to deconstruct media."

"Tame Your Family's Media Before it Takes Over Your Lives!" from Educate and Empower Kid
This article suggests 3 simple ways to help your family be media healthy. These tips can help you manage your media, so it doesn't manage you!

"Why A Family Tech Detox is Just What the Doctor Ordered" from Educate and Empower Kid
Food detoxing has become very popular; this article discusses why media detoxes are just as important, and gives 5 simple steps to help you do it!

26. Body Image

How we feel about our appearance can really affect how we feel about our entire selves. Often we think this is just something that girls and women struggle with, but many men are self-conscious of their looks as well.

This is a topic that parents need to be particularly wise as they approach it. You do NOT want to suggest to your child that they specifically will become dissatisfied with their appearance. But your child should know that ALL of us can be highly affected by the many voices around us, whether those are from family members, friends, relatives, movies, social media, etc.

Lesson #25, "Being Media Savvy," and our books focusing on healthy body image, *Messages About Me: Sydney's Story* and *Messages About Me: Wade's Story*, will be very helpful in these discussions. Helping your child to develop a healthy body image will also help improve their overall self-worth!

Start the Conversation
Start by discussing how our culture absurdly places so much emphasis on physical appearance when we have no control over the appearance we were born with. As you talk about healthy body image with your child, explain the importance of accepting and liking one's body just the way it is and striving for real physical health. Talks about ways your family is maintaining good health

"Comparison with myself brings improvement, comparison with others brings discontent."

—BETTY JAMIE CHUNG

Teach your child that they decide their worth, not the media or anybody else. Explain that they will be bombarded by photoshopped, digitized images for the rest of their lives. Because of that, they must learn to look at every image logically. They will need to remind themselves that all media, including social media, are full of fake images with impossible physical standards that no one can attain—not even the people in them.

Show your child that they are worthwhile simply because they exist. Behaving in ways that can make them proud of themselves is so much more important than how the world thinks they should look.

Questions for Your Child

- What do you like about your personality, your abilities, and how your brain works?
- What do you like about the way you look?
- How does the way you view your body affect the way you feel about yourself as a whole?
- When we spend a lot of time watching TV, YouTube videos, or scrolling through social media, we often compare ourselves to other people. We might feel like everyone else has more stuff than we do or is better looking than us. What can we do to combat these negative feelings?

and what all of you can do to improve your health (meditation, yoga, eating more fruits and vegetables, playing games outside more, etc.)

Most importantly, help your child appreciate all their bodies can DO, like jump, sing, learn, laugh, cry, and so much more. Ask your child to name at least 10 things their body can do and then talk about how these things are far more important than one's looks.

- Do you think the people on TV look like the people we know in real life?
- Why is being concerned about being a good person more important than worrying about the way we look?
- How might our body image affect how we behave in relationships?

Activity

Have each person in your family share at least two things that he or she likes or loves about every other person in your family. Have one person write down on separate pieces of paper what was said about each family member. Each person must also write down at least two things they like about themselves on this list. Instruct each family member to hang up the list that was recorded somewhere where they can see it daily.

Additional Resources:

"Teaching Our Kids about Healthy Body Image" from Educate and Empower Kids
This lesson includes great advice to help you teach your child to have a more positive body image.

"Positive Body Image Starts With Moms" from Educate and Empower Kids
This article discusses how the way that mothers feel about their own bodies will influence the way that their children think they should feel about their own bodies.

"Teaching Healthy Body Image to Boys" from Educate and Empower Kids
Includes a lesson for parents that is geared specifically towards helping parents teach their young boys about developing a healthy body image.

"Teaching Kids About Healthy Body Image: Tips from the Experts" from Educate and Empower Kids
Studies show that kids, on average, are viewing media for about 8 hours a day. Is it any wonder distorted body image views are so common amongst our children?

27. Self Worth & Self Esteem

Each and every person is completely unique and special. It is so important for our kids to understand that each person has importance, worth, and purpose. Explain to your kids that a person who has healthy self-worth behaves differently from someone who does not. A person who is proud of themselves and can admire their own behavior will NOT do or ask others to do things that make them uncomfortable.

Our book *30 Days to a Stronger Child* is a great resource with amazing family night discussions on self-confidence, empathy, assertiveness, positive self-talk, as well as other topics related to our intellectual, spiritual, physical, social, and emotional health.

Start the Conversation

Help separate your child's appearance from his or her self-worth. Describe some of the actions a person who doesn't feel good about themselves might take: he might be sad, she might tease others, he might hide his body, she might show too much of her body to get attention, etc. A person with self-respect is confident, kind, and won't do anything intentionally to hurt others or make them feel uncomfortable. Ask your child how a person's dress, demeanor, facial expressions, language, and actions are reflections of how they feel about themselves. Most importantly, teach your child that comparing themselves to others is unproductive and does not lead to true self-worth!

Questions for Your Child

- There is no one else in the whole universe that is the same as you. Why are each of us different and special?
- How are you special to our family?
- What are your talents and skills?
- What can you do to make the world a better place?
- How might a person who feels good about themselves act differently from someone who does not?
- Where do you find your worth? What qualities do you admire in yourself?
- How does one's self-worth affect the way they treat others?
- How might self-worth affect their decision to enter a relationship or have sex?

Activity

Make a list of all the things you can think of that make YOU wonderful inside and out. Think about the unique way you sleep, eat, walk, run, do homework, make friends, play games, talk with others, write stories, etc. Think about your unique tastes in books, movies, friends, foods, and whatever else you like. What makes you YOU? Have each member of your family make a list and then share them with one another.

> "Low self-confidence isn't a life sentence. Self-confidence can be learned, practiced, and mastered--just like any other skill. Once you master it, everything in your life will change for the better."
>
> -Barrie Davenport

Additional Resources:

"5 Ways A Mother Can Develop Self-Worth In Her Son" from Educate and Empower Kids
This article offers mothers a variety of ways that they can help their sons develop positive self-worth.

"I Love Myself and That's What Makes Me Beautiful" from Educate and Empower Kids
This article gives tips on how to love yourself and teach your children to learn to love themselves. Don't rely on others to do it for you!

"5 Things A Father Can Do to Increase His Daughter's Self-Worth" from Educate and Empower Kids
This article describes a number of ways that fathers can help their daughters to develop positive self-worth.

"Empower Your Child Today Through Positive Self-Talk and Affirmations" from Educate and Empower Kids
You can nourish your child's view of themselves with a simple solution: compliment them! And teach them affirmations to help them realize their worth!

"Learning Positive Self-Talk" from Educate and Empower Kids
Children need to know that their self-worth is based on who they are, not how they fit into popular culture. This lesson can help you do just that!

28.
Shame & Guilt

Helping kids understand the difference between shame and guilt is something that will not only help them in their sexual education, but in their emotional education as well. Remember, guilt is the idea, "I made a mistake." Shame is the idea, "I am a terrible person." Guilt can lead to making amends, and creating lasting change in our lives. Shame is often associated with lower self-worth, depression, and anxiety.

Point out that some people think sex is bad or dirty. Teach your children that this is a sad myth. Sex is not bad. It is wonderful and healthy! However, some people feel embarrassed about sex, their own bodies, and other things related to sex, so they make others feel ashamed about it as well. Remind your kids sex is a normal, natural act for adults.

Start the Conversation
Sexual intercourse is a very intimate act that often happens naked, which can make people feel vulnerable, sometimes leading to feelings of guilt and shame. Explain the difference between guilt and shame. Ask your child what situations could cause shame about sex.

Use the glossary to discuss consent and sexual assault. Help your child understand that sexual assault is against the law and that the abuser should feel terrible for what they've done, and need to be punished accordingly. However, sexual assault often causes the victim to feel shame and guilt, but an assault is NEVER the victim's fault! Teach your child that if anything abusive ever happens to them they need not feel ashamed.

Questions for Your Child
- Why might guilt be a good thing?
- What is the difference between guilt and shame?

> "If you put shame in a petri dish, it needs three ingredients to grow exponentially: secrecy, silence, and judgment. If you put the same amount of shame in the petri dish and douse it with empathy, it can't survive."
>
> -Brené Brown

- When we have made a mistake, how can we stop ourselves from feeling shame and instead focus on what we can do to make things better and move forward?
- Sometimes kids and adults who have been sexually abused feel shame or blame themselves for what was done to them. Why do you think this happens?
- What have you learned about sex that can help you to have a positive attitude toward it?
- Why do some people feel shameful or guilty about sex?
- What can you do if you feel guilty or ashamed about something you have done or seen?

Activity

Write down the following scenarios on small pieces of paper and pass out one or more to each family member. Ask your children what the person is feeling (shame or guilt), and if they should feel ashamed or guilty for their actions. If not, what can they do to work through their feelings?

- Sarah calls her brother a cruel name. Afterward she thinks, "I always overreact with him. I'm such a jerk."
- Billy strikes out while at bat. At first he feels like he's let his team down, but then takes a deep breath and relaxes.
- Charlie drops a stack of dishes. He says, "Ugh, why am I always so clumsy?"
- Nora didn't study for her test and gets a bad grade. Feeling upset, she thinks, "I should have studied. That was a big mistake."

Additional Resources:

"Three Mistakes I've Made Using Shame and Guilt" from Educate and Empower Kids
This article describes some of the ways parents may inadvertently teach their children to associate shame and guilt with body image and behavior.

"30 Days to a Stronger Child" from Educate and Empower Kids
This book provides 30 lessons to help you out as you work to teach your child what they need to know to have positive self worth and live a healthy, balanced, and strong life.

"Raising Strong Kids in a Porn Culture" from Educate and Empower Kids
This video, from the Utah Coalition Against Pornography Conference, discusses small, simple habits to build resilience in our children and teens against pornography and other negative influences.

29. Pregnancy

Describe conception and pregnancy. As you discuss these, add any additional information you think your child may need. This may also be a good time to discuss infertility, adoption, and abortion. Feel free to discuss your cultural and spiritual beliefs in regards to pregnancy and birth control. You may also wish to discuss alternative methods of becoming pregnant or becoming parents such as in vitro fertilization, intrauterine insemination, surrogacy, and adoption.

Check the glossary for any definitions you may need such as uterus, vagina, penis, fertilize, gestation, abstinence, contraceptive, the pill, condom, etc.

Start the Conversation

Explain to your child that although sex is usually required for someone to get pregnant, one does not become pregnant every time she has sex. Although seemingly commonplace and "natural," the act of reproduction represents somewhat of a miracle in the creation of a new person. Since it only takes one sperm to fertilize an egg, pregnancy can occur even if there is no ejaculation. Any vaginal, sexual intercourse can cause a pregnancy. Then explain how conception works:

When a man ejaculates, millions of sperm are propelled into the vagina. From there, the sperm must swim through the vagina and the cervix and up the fallopian tube. Only a few dozen sperm may actually make it to the egg. The fastest and strongest sperm can make the trip in around 45 minutes, but fertilization can occur up to a week after sex. Once the sperm reaches the egg, there is a frantic effort to get through the cell wall. The first one in causes a cellular reaction making the fertilized egg impenetrable to any other sperm. The fertilized egg is now an embryo. At the instant of fertilization, the baby's genes and sex are set. If the sperm has a Y chromosome, your baby will be a boy. If it has an X chromosome, the baby will be a girl.

The fertilized egg stays in the fallopian tube for about 3 to 4 days, but within 24 hours of being fertilized, it quickly starts dividing into many cells. It keeps dividing as it moves slowly through the fallopian tube to the uterus. Its next job is to attach to the lining of the uterus. This is called implantation. During pregnancy, the embryo or fetus grows and develops inside a woman's uterus. A full-term pregnancy lasts approximately 40 weeks.

If no sperm is around to fertilize the egg, it passes through to the uterus and disintegrates. A woman's hormone levels then go back to normal and her body sheds the thick lining of the uterus, and her period starts.

Questions for Your Child

- What other physical changes happen to a woman's body during pregnancy?
- Do you know how to prevent pregnancy?
- Pregnancies can be difficult and painful. Why would women choose to have a baby?
- What are the blessings that come from having a child?
- Are there advantages to a child who is born in a family with two committed, married parents?
- Let's review lesson #7; do you remember how a woman becomes pregnant?

Activity

Talk about some of the funny, strange, and difficult experiences with yours or your spouse's pregnancy. Explain some of the joy, fear, and wonder you felt at carrying and giving birth to a child. Show your child photos or videos of the day they were born. Express your love and gratitude that your child came into your family.

Additional Resources:

"Common Questions Kids Ask About Sex (And How to Answer)" from Educate and Empower Kids
"We want our kids to be curious about life, and we want them to ask us their questions. However, talking to our children about sex and questions that surround sex can sometimes be scary or nerve-wracking."

"4 Easy Steps to Creating Healthy Communication About Sexual Intimacy" from Educate and Empower Kids
"When we make it clear to our children that we will talk to them about anything–no boundaries–we encourage them to come to us, rather than plunging down the wormhole of the internet..."

"7 Steps to Take to Establish Yourself as an Approachable Parent" from Educate and Empower Kids
"...the advice I am most comfortable doling out, is to prioritize becoming an approachable parent. In other words, you want to learn how to listen to your kids talk about sex, not just learn what to say to them about sex."

30. STDs & STIs

There are many kinds of sexually transmitted diseases (STDs) and sexually transmitted infections (STIs). Use the glossary to help you discuss some or all of these with your kids. Be specific and teach your children how these can be spread through vaginal, anal, and oral sex. (See the glossary for definitions.)

Teach your kids how to prevent STDs and STIs, and discuss how one can find out if they have been infected and where one could get tested.

Start the Conversation

Ask your child if he has heard of AIDS, HIV, HPV, herpes, syphilis, hepatitis B or C, chlamydia, pubic lice, and/or gonorrhea. Use the glossary to help you define these. Explain that these are all sexually transmitted infections or diseases and that some of them are deadly. Others won't kill, but will stay in the body for life.

Talk about the best ways to avoid STIs and STDs, like abstinence, monogamy, and condom use. Many people have begun transitioning from using the term STD to using STI in an effort to clarify that not all sexually transmitted infections turn into a disease.

 STD: *An abbreviation that refers to sexually transmitted diseases. These are illnesses that are communicable through sexual behaviors, including intercourse. Some of these illnesses can also be transmitted through blood contact.*

Questions for Your Child

Q What are sexually transmitted diseases (STDs) and sexually transmitted infections (STIs)? Do you understand how they are spread?

Q Why are these diseases harmful? Which ones are incurable?

Q How does avoiding sex until you are in a fully committed relationship or marriage keep you safer from STDs?

Q How are diseases and infections spread? How are STDs and STIs different from colds, flu, warts, and other illnesses? (These other illnesses are spread through human contact and bodily fluid, but STIs and STDs are transmitted through sexual contact with an infected person.)

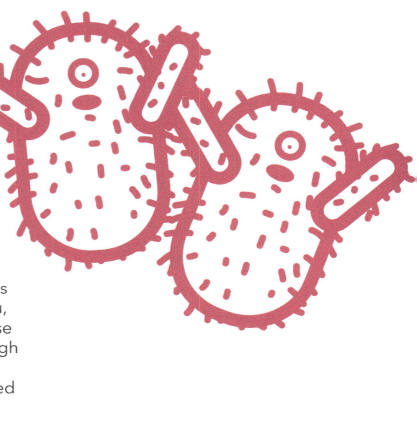

Additional Resources:

"Information for Teens And Young Adults: Staying Healthy and Preventing STDs" from the CDC
This page provides helpful information from the Center for Disease Control on how to prevent STDs and how to practice safe sex.

"Holding Family Meetings: A Necessity for Our Busy Families" from Educate and Empower Kids
Knowing how to hold a family meeting where all can share and relate to one another is one of the best ways to open those lines of communication, and this article can help you do that.

"Adolescents and Young Adults" from the CDC
This page provides links to videos and other resources about how to talk to your child about these topics and gives more information on STDs.

"Sexually Transmitted Infections (STIs)" from the WHO
This article from the World Health Organization goes into greater depth on statistics about sexually transmitted infections, and how to prevent, diagnose, and treat them.

TOPIC CARDS

CUT OUT THESE TOPIC CARDS TO HELP YOU START TALKING!
Post one on your refrigerator to remind yourself,
or to let your kids know, of the upcoming discussion.

1. PUBLIC VS PRIVATE

- Why are some topics private?
- I can ask my parents difficult questions.
- My home is a safe zone.
- Is it okay to discuss sex with another adult who are not my parents?

2. MALE ANATOMY

- Penis
- Testicle/Scrotum
- Anus

3. FEMALE ANATOMY

- Vagina
- Urethra
- Anus
- Nipples/Breast

4. PUBERTY FOR BOYS

- Physical changes: hair growth, sweat, voice changes
- Emotional changes
- Nocturnal emissions (or "wet dreams")
- Spontaneous erection

5. PUBERTY FOR GIRLS

- Physical changes: hair growth, sweat breast development
- Emotional changes
- Feelings of arousal, wetness and discharge in vaginal area are normal

6. MENSTURAL CYCLE

- Age of first menstruation varies widely. Average age is 12
- Egg is released monthly
- Discharge (mucus from vagina) may begin about 6 months before first period

7. PHYSICAL MECHANICS OF SEXUAL INTERCOURSE

- Erection
- Feelings of arousal in the clitoris and wetness in the vaginal area
- Penis is inserted into vagina
- Sperm is released from penis

8. EMOTIONAL ASPECTS OF SEX

- Sex can be a natural expression of emotional love.
- Can create feelings of hurt and confusion if not accompanied by love.
- Sex can be a binding force in a relationship.

9. RELATIONSHIPS ARE GOOD & WONDERFUL

- Monogamy
- Emotional & spiritual benefits of monogamy
- Health benefits of monogramy

10. WHAT DOES A HEALTHY RELATIONSHIP LOOK LIKE

- A healthy relationship includes good communication
- It is not okay to hurt another person
- Abuse can be emotional, mental, and/or physical
- Both people in a relationship deserve respect & dignity

11. ROMANTIC LOVE

- What is romantic love?
- How is this different from other kinds of love?
- How do people show romantic love?

12. DIFFERENT KINDS OF FAMILIES

- There are many different kinds of families
- Some kids are raised by grandparents, aunts, uncles, or other members of families
- Some kids are raised by a single parent
- Some kids are raised by two dads or two moms
- Some kids are raised by one dad and one mom

13. GENDER & GENDER ROLES

- Are there typical boy & girl interests?
- It's okay for boys & girls to pursue whatever activities they are interested in doing.
- Don't let stereotypical gender roles stop you from trying something new.

14. SEXUAL IDENTIFICATION

- It is individual & unique
- Loving your friends is different from being "in love"
- Your sexuality is an integral part of you but it does not define who you are.
- Be careful not to have your sexuality defined for you by outside influences (friends, media, etc)

15. AT WHAT AGE IS SOMEONE READY FOR A SEXUAL RELATIONSHIP?

- Stages of a sexual relationship: handholding, hugging, kissing, petting, sex
- People are ready for these stages at different ages
- Children are not physically or emotionally ready for a sexual relationship

16. CURIOUSITY

- Curiousity about sex, your developing body, and other's bodies is completely normal.
- Children should never feel ashamed for being curious.
- It's important to know who to talk to about your curiousity & questions
- Parents are the best source of information and won't make you feel ashamed.

17. MASTURBATION

- Masturbation is self-stimulation of the genitals
- Some people do it to achieve orgasm
- Is it okay for kids?

18. CHILDREN DO NOT HAVE SEX

- Children's bodies are not ready for sex
- Children are not emotionally ready for sex.
- You always have the right to say "NO!"

19. WHAT TO DO IF SOMETHING HAS HAPPENED TO YOU - WHO TO TALK TO

- A child should always tell someone right away if they have ever been touched in a way that makes them uncomfortable
- Who should you talk to if someone touches you in this way
- Trustworthy people could include doctors, police officers, & parents
- Not even trusted adults should make you feel uncomfortable
- You won't be in trouble and you will be believed.

20. HOW PREDATORS GROOM CHILDREN

- What does it mean for predators to groom children for sexual molestation/abuse?
- Predators are often people the child knows.
- Listen to your instincts
- Children should never keep secrets from their parents about sex.

21. HOW TO SAY "NO!"

- You can say NO to anyone
- When is it very important to say NO to someone?
- Practice saying NO loudly and firmly
- Even if you have done something in the past, doesn't me you have to do it again.

22. YOUR INSTINCTS KEEP YOU SAFE

- Instincts are apart of us and can keep us safe.
- Instincts can help us make good decisions.
- What does that "icky" feeling mean? Have you ever had that "icky" feeling?

23. PORNOGRAPHY

- What is pornography?
- Have you ever seen something that was pornographic?
- Pornography is damaging to individuals, relationships & society
- Develop a plan for what to do if your child is exposed to pornography

24. SEXTING & SOCIAL MEDIA

- What are sexually explicit messages?
- Even an innocent receiver of a nude picture can get in trouble for having it.
- People have used sexting images to get other people in trouble.
- Discuss the rules of your house for using social media and cell phones.
- Why do you think these rules are important?
- What should you do if you receive sexual messages/images online or on your phone?

25. BEING MEDIA SAVVY

- Media can influence your body image if you allow it.
- The people in media image are almost always altered by airbrushing or photoshopping.
- We don't all fall into a single definition of beauty because people are all different shapes and sizes.

26. BODY IMAGE

- Developing a healthy body image improves our self-esteem
- How does body image affect your sense of inherent value as a human being?
- How do you see yourself?

27. SELF-ESTEEM SELF-WORTH

- A person who has healthy self-worth behaves differently than a person who does not.
- A person with healthy self-esteem will not do or ask others to do things that make them feel uncomfortable.
- Think about the things that make you unique.
- You are worth more than what your body can do.

28. SHAME & GUILT

- Some people think sex is bad or dirty, this is a sad myth.
- What situations could cause guilt about sex?
- Sexual assault can cause a victim to feel shame or guilt, but an assault is never a victim's fault

29. PREGNANCY

- Sperm from male fertilizes egg in female.
- Egg travels from fallopian tube to uterus.
- Fertilized egg is now an embryo.
- A full term pregnancy lasts approximately 40 weeks.

30. STDs & STIs

- There are many kinds of STDs and STIs.
- Some STDs and STIs last a lifetime.
- Prevention includes abstinence, followed by monogamy, and regular condom use.

GLOSSARY

The following terms have been included to assist you as you prepare and hold discussions with your children regarding healthy sexuality and intimacy. The definitions are not intended for the child; rather, they are meant to clarify the concepts and terms for the adult. Some terms may not be appropriate for your child, given their age, circumstances, or your own family culture and values. Use your judgment to determine which terminology best meets your individual needs.

Abortion: An abortion is a procedure to end a pregnancy. It uses medicine and/or surgery to remove the embryo or fetus and placenta from the uterus.

Abstinence: The practice of not doing or having something that is wanted or enjoyable; the practice of abstaining from something.

Abuse: The improper usage or treatment of another person or entity, often to unfairly gain power and/or other benefit in the relationship.

Affection: A feeling of liking or caring for something or someone. A type of love that surpasses general goodwill.

AIDS: A sexually transmitted or bloodborne viral infection that causes immune deficiency.

Anal Sex: A form of intercourse that generally involves the insertion and thrusting of the erect penis into the anus and rectum for sexual pleasure.

Anus: The external opening of the rectum, composed of two sphincters which control the exit of feces from the body.

Appropriate: Suitable, proper, or fitting for a particular purpose, person, or circumstance.

Arousal (in regards to sexual activities): The physical and emotional response to sexual desire during or in anticipation of sexual activity. In men, this results in an erection. In women, arousal results in vaginal lubrication (wetness), engorgement of the external genitals (clitoris and labia), and enlargement of the vagina.

Birth Control: The practice of preventing unwanted pregnancies, especially by use of contraception. See also IUD, condom, contraceptive implant, and the pill.

Birth Control Shot: Commonly referred to as the birth control shot, Depo-Provera® is an injectable form of birth control. This contraceptive option is a shot that contains the hormone progesterone and is given on a regular schedule.

Bisexual: A sexual orientation in which one is attracted to both males and females.

Body Image: An individual's feelings regarding their own physical appearance, attractiveness, and/or sexuality. These feelings and opinions are often influenced by other people and media sources.

Bodily Integrity: The personal belief that our bodies, while crucial to our understanding of who we are, do not in themselves solely define our worth. The knowledge that our bodies are the storehouse of our humanity, and the sense that we esteem our bodies and we treat them accordingly. It is also defined as the right to autonomy and self-determination over one's own body.

Boundaries: The personal limits or guidelines that an individual forms in order to clearly identify what are reasonable and safe behaviors for others to engage in around him or her.

Bowel Movement: Also known as defecation, a bowel movement is the final act of digestion by which waste is eliminated from the body via the anus.

Breasts: Breasts contain mammary glands, which create the breast milk used to feed infants. Women develop breasts on their upper torso during puberty.

Child: A term often used in reference to individuals who are under the age of 18. This overlaps with the term "teen."

Circumcision: The surgical removal of foreskin from a baby's penis.

Chlamydia: A common sexually transmitted infection caused by the bacteria chlamydia trachomatis. It can affect the eyes and may cause damage to a woman's reproductive system.

Clitoris: A female sex organ visible at the front juncture of the labia minora above the opening of the urethra. The clitoris is the female's most sensitive erogenous zone.

Condom: A thin rubber covering that a man wears on his penis during sex in order to prevent a woman from becoming pregnant and/or to help prevent the spread of diseases.

Consent: Clear agreement or permission to do something. Consent must be given freely, without force or intimidation, while the person is fully conscious and cognizant of their present situation.

Contraceptive: A method, device, or medication that works to prevent pregnancy. Another name for birth control. See birth control, IUD, condom, or diaphragm.

Contraceptive Implant: A long-term birth control option for women. A contraceptive implant is a flexible plastic rod about the size of a matchstick that is placed under the skin of the upper arm.

Curiosity: The desire to learn or know more about something or someone.

Date Rape: A rape that is committed by someone with a person they have gone on a date with. The perpetrator uses physical force, psychological intimidation, and/or drugs or alcohol to force the victim to have sex either against their will or in a state in which they cannot give clear consent.

Degrade: To treat with contempt or disrespect.

Demean: To cause a severe loss in dignity or respect in another person.

Derogatory: An adjective that implies severe criticism or loss of respect.

Diaphragm (Contraceptive): A cervical barrier type of birth control made of a soft latex or silicone dome with a spring molded into the rim. The spring creates a seal against the walls of the vagina, preventing semen, including sperm, from entering the fallopian tubes.

Domestic Abuse/Domestic Violence: A pattern of abusive behavior in any relationship that is used by one partner to gain and/or maintain power and control over another in a domestic setting. It can be physical, sexual, emotional, economic, and/or psychological actions or threats of actions that harm another person. (From the Department of Justice.)

Double Standard: A rule or standard that is applied differently and/or unfairly to a person or distinct groups of people.

Egg Cell/Ovum: The female reproductive cell, which, when fertilized by sperm, will eventually grow into an infant.

Ejaculation: When a man reaches orgasm and semen is expelled from the penis.

Emotion: An emotion is a feeling such as happiness, love, fear, sadness, or anger, which can be caused by the situation that you are in or the people you are with.

Emotional Abuse: A form of abuse in which another person is subjected to behavior that can result in psychological trauma. Emotional abuse often occurs within relationships where there is a power imbalance.

Emotional Intimacy: A form of intimacy that displays a degree of closeness which focuses more on the emotional over the physical aspects of a relationship.

Epididymal Hypertension: A condition that results from prolonged sexual arousal in human males in which fluid congestion in the testicles occurs, often accompanied by testicular pain. The condition is temporary, and is also referred to as "blue balls."

Erection: When the penis becomes engorged/enlarged with blood, often as a result of sexual arousal.

Explicit: In reference to sexual content, "sexually explicit" is meant to signify that the content with such a warning will portray sexual content openly and clearly to the viewers.

Extortion: To obtain something through force or threats, particularly sex or money.

Family: A group consisting of parents and children living together in a household. The definition of family is constantly evolving, and every person can define family in a different way to encompass the relationships they share with people in their life. Over time one's family will change as one's life changes and the importance of family values and rituals deepen.

Female Arousal: The physiological responses to sexual desire during or in anticipation of sexual activity in women. This includes vaginal lubrication (wetness), engorgement of the external genitals (clitoris and labia), enlargement of the vagina, and dilation of the pupils.

Fertilize: The successful union between an egg (ovum) and a sperm, which normally occurs within the second portion of the fallopian tube, also known as the ampulla. The result of fertilization is a zygote (fertilized egg).

Forced Affection: Pressuring or forcing a child to give a hug, kiss, or any other form of physical affection when they do not have the desire to do so.

Foreskin: The fold of skin which covers the head (the glans) of the penis. Also called the prepuce.

Friend: Someone with whom a person has a relationship of mutual affection and is typically closer than an associate or acquaintance.

Gay: A slang term used to describe people who are sexually attracted to members of the same sex. The term "lesbian" is generally used when talking about women who are attracted to other women. Originally, the word "gay" meant "carefree"; its connection to sexual orientation developed during the latter half of the 20th century.

Gender: Masculinity and femininity are differentiated through a range of characteristics known as "gender." However, use of this term may include biological sex (being male or female), social roles based upon biological sex, and/or one's subjective experience and understanding of their own gender identity.

Gender Role: The commonly perceived pattern of masculine or feminine behavior as defined by an individual's culture and/or upbringing.

Gender Stereotypes: A generalized thought or understanding applied to either males or females (or other gender identities) that may or may not correspond with reality. "Men don't cry" or "women are weak" are examples of inaccurate gender stereotypes.

Gestation: The period of time when a person or animal is developing inside its mother's womb preparing to be born.

Gonorrhea: A sexually transmitted disease that affects both males and females, usually the rectum, throat, and/or urethra. It can also infect the cervix in females.

Grooming (Predatory): To prepare/train and/or desensitize someone, usually a child, with the intent of committing a sexual offense and/or harm.

Healthy Sexuality: Having the ability to express one's sexuality in ways that contribute positively to one's own self-esteem and relationships. Healthy sexuality includes approaching sexual relationships and interactions with mutual agreement and dignity. It must include mutual respect and a lack of fear, shame, or guilt and never include coercion or violence.

Hepatitis B: Hepatitis B (HBV) is an incurable disease which is most commonly spread through exposure to infected bodily fluids via unclean needles, unscreened blood, and/or sexual content. It can manifest as acute or chronic. The acute form can resolve itself in less than six months, but it will often turn chronic. The chronic form can persist in the body for a lifetime and lead to a number of serious illnesses including cirrhosis and liver cancer. The younger a person is exposed to HBV, the more likely it will become chronic.

Hepatitis C: Similarly transmitted to Hepatitis B, Hepatitis C attacks the liver. Though most individuals with Hepatitis C are asymptomatic, individuals who do develop symptoms typically show signs of yellowing skin and eyes, fatigue, and/or nausea.

Herpes: A series of diseases of the skin caused by the herpes virus which cause sores and inflammation of the skin. Type 1 viruses will manifest as cold sores on the lips or nose, while the type 2 viruses are sexually transmitted and specifically known as genital herpes. This causes painful sores on the genital area.

Heterosexual: Sexual orientation in which one is attracted to members of the opposite sex (males are attracted to females; females are attracted to males). See also, straight.

HIV: HIV (human immunodeficiency virus) is a virus that attacks the body's immune system. If not treated, it will turn into AIDS. It is incurable and will persist in the body for life. It is spread through infected bodily fluids and sexual contact.

Homosexual: Sexual orientation in which one is attracted to members of the same sex (males are attracted to males; females are attracted to females). See also gay or lesbian.

Hookup Sex: A form of casual sex in which sexual activity takes place outside the context of a committed relationship. The sex may be a one-time event, or an ongoing arrangement. In either case, the focus is generally on the physical enjoyment of sexual activity without an emotional involvement or commitment.

HPV: Human papillomavirus. It is the most common STD in the United States and can cause genital warts or cancer in about 10% of those infected. Anyone over age 10 can receive the vaccine for HPV.

Hymen: A membrane that partially closes the opening of the vagina and whose presence is traditionally taken to be a mark of virginity. However, it can often be broken before a woman has sex simply by being active, and sometimes it is not present at all.

Hyper-sexualized: To make extremely sexual; to emphasize the sexuality of. Often seen in media.

Instinct: An inherent response or inclination toward a particular behavior. An action or reaction that is performed without being based on prior experience.

Intercourse: Sexual activity, also known as coitus or copulation, that most commonly understood to refer to the insertion of the penis into the vagina (vaginal sex). It should be noted that there are a wide range of various sexual activities and the boundaries of what constitutes sexual intercourse are still under debate. See also, sex.

Intersex: An umbrella term used to refer to the rare phenomenom of an individual born with some mixture of both male and female reproductive anatomy. This can be very obvious with visibly deformed or underdeveloped reproductive organs, to something as subtle as alterations in the xy chromosomes. It's also possible for signs of intersex to not develop until later in life.

Intimacy: Generally, a feeling or form of significant closeness. There are four types of intimacy: physical intimacy (sensual proximity or touching), emotional intimacy (close connection resulting from trust and love), cognitive or intellectual intimacy (resulting from honest exchange of thoughts and ideas), and experiential intimacy (a connection that occurs while working together). Emotional and physical intimacy are often associated with sexual relationships, while intellectual and experiential intimacy are not. However, people can engage in a sexual experience that is devoid of intmacy.

IUD: A small, T-shaped device that is placed in the uterus to prevent pregnancy.

Labia: The inner and outer folds of the vulva on both sides of the vagina.

Lesbian: A word used to describe women who are sexually attracted to other women.

Lice (Pubic): A sexually transmitted sucking louse infesting the pubic region of the human body.

Love: A wide range of emotional interpersonal connections, feelings, and attitudes. Common forms include kinship or familial love, friendship, divine love (as demonstrated through worship), and sexual or romantic love. In biological terms, love is the attraction and bonding that functions to unite human beings and facilitate the social and sexual continuation of the species.

Masturbation: Self-stimulation of the genitals in order to produce sexual arousal, pleasure, and/or orgasm.

Media Literacy: The ability to study, interpret, and create messages in various media such as books, social media posts, online ads, movies, etc. It also includes understanding how to navigate being online, what to avoid, and what information to share and/or keep private.

Menstrual Cycle: The egg is released from ovaries through the fallopian tube into the uterus. Each month, a lining of blood and tissue build up in the uterus. When the egg is not fertilized, this lining is no longer needed and is shed from the body through the vagina. The cycle is roughly 28 days, but can vary between individuals. The bleeding lasts around 2-7 days. The menstrual cycle may be accompanied by cramping, breast tenderness, and emotional sensitivity.

Menstrual Period: A discharging of blood, secretions, and tissue debris from the uterus as it sheds its thickened lining (endometrium) approximately once per month in females who've reached a fertile age. This does not occur during pregnancy.

Misandry: Like misogyny, it is the hatred, aversion, hostility, or dislike of men or boys. Similarly, it also can appear in a single individual, or may also be manifest in broad cultural trends.

Misogyny: The hatred, aversion, hostility, or dislike of women or girls. Misogyny can appear in a single individual, or may also be manifest in broad cultural trends that undermine women's autonomy and value.

Molestation: Aggressive and persistent harassment, either psychological or physical, of a sexual manner.

Monogamy: A relationship in which a person has one partner at any one time.

Nipples: The circular, somewhat conical structure of tissue on the breast. The skin of the nipple and its surrounding areola are often several shades darker than that of the surrounding breast tissue. In women, the nipple delivers breast milk to infants.

Nocturnal Emissions: A spontaneous orgasm that occurs during sleep. Nocturnal emissions can occur in both males (ejaculation) and females (lubrication of the vagina). The term "wet dream" is often used to describe male nocturnal emissions.

Non-binary/Genderqueer: Non-binary or genderqueer is an umbrella term for gender identities that are neither male nor female—identities that are outside the gender binary. Non-binary identities fall under the transgender umbrella, since non-binary people typically identify with a gender that is different from their assigned sex.

Nudity: The state of not wearing any clothing. Full nudity denotes a complete absence of clothing, while partial nudity is a more ambiguous term, denoting the presence of an indeterminate amount of clothing.

Oral Sex: Sexual activity that involves stimulation of the genitals through the use of another person's mouth.

Orgasm: The rhythmic muscular contractions in the pelvic region that occur as a result of sexual stimulation, arousal, and activity during the sexual response cycle. Orgasms are characterized by a sudden release of built-up sexual tension and the resulting sexual pleasure.

Penis: The external, male sexual organ comprised of the shaft, foreskin, glans penis, and meatus. The penis contains the urethra, through which both urine and semen travel to exit the body.

Perception: A way of regarding, understanding, or interpreting something; a mental impression.

Period: The beginning of the menstrual cycle.

Physical Abuse: The improper physical treatment of another person with the intent to cause bodily harm, pain, or other suffering. Physical abuse is often employed to unfairly gain power or other benefit in the relationship.

The Pill: An oral contraceptive for women containing the hormones estrogen and progesterone or progesterone alone. This prevents ovulation, fertilization, or implantation of a fertilized ovum, causing temporary infertility.

Polyamory: The practice of engaging in multiple romantic (and typically sexual) relationships, with the agreement of all the people involved.

Pornography: The portrayal of explicit sexual content for the purpose of causing sexual arousal. In it, sex and bodies are commodified for the purpose of making a financial profit. It can be created in a variety of media contexts, including videos, photos, animation, books, and magazines. Its most lucrative means of distribution is through the internet. The industry that creates pornography is a sophisticated, corporatized, billion-dollar business.

Positive Self-Talk: Anything said to oneself for encouragement or motivation, such as phrases or mantras; also, one's ongoing internal conversation with oneself, like a running commentary, which influences how one feels and behaves.

(Sexual) Predator: Someone who seeks to obtain sexual contact/ pleasure from another through predatory and/or abusive behavior. The term is often used to describe the deceptive and coercive methods used by people who commit sex crimes with a victim.

Pregnancy: The common term used for gestation in humans. During pregnancy, the embryo or fetus grows and develops inside a woman's uterus.

Premature Ejaculation: When a man regularly reaches orgasm, during which semen is expelled from the penis, prior to or within one minute of the initiation of sexual activity.

Priapism: The technical term of a condition in which the erect penis does not return to flaccidity within four hours, despite the absence of physical or psychological sexual stimulation.

Private: Belonging to or for the use of a specific individual. Private and privacy denote a state of being alone, solitary, individual, exclusive, secret, personal, hidden, and confidential.

Psychological Abuse: A form of abuse where the abuser regularly uses a range of actions or words with the intent to manipulate, weaken, or confuse a person's thoughts. This distorts the victim's sense of self and harms their mental wellbeing. Psychological abuse often occurs within relationships in which there is a power imbalance.

Puberty: A period or process through which children reach sexual maturity. Once a person has reached puberty, their body is capable of sexual reproduction.

Public: Belonging to or for the use of all people in a specific area, or all people as a whole. Something that is public is common, shared, collective, communal, and widespread.

Queer: A historically derogatory term against people who were homosexual, that has been reclaimed by the LGBTQ+ community. It is also an umbrella term for sexual and gender minorities who are not heterosexual.

Rape: A sex crime in which the perpetrator forces another person to have sexual intercourse against their will and without consent. Rape often occurs through the threat or actuality of violence against the victim.

Rape Culture: A culture in which rape is pervasive and, to an extent, normalized due to cultural and societal attitudes towards gender and sexuality. Behaviors that facilitate rape culture include victim blaming, sexual objectification, and denial regarding sexual violence.

Relationship: The state of being connected, united, or related to another person.

Rhythm Method: A method of avoiding pregnancy by restricting sexual intercourse to the times of a woman's menstrual cycle when ovulation and conception are least likely to occur. Because it can be difficult to predict ovulation, the effectiveness of the rhythm method is on average just 75-87%.

Romantic Love: A form of love that denotes intimacy and a strong desire for emotional connection with another person to whom one is generally also sexually attracted.

Scrotum: The pouch of skin underneath the penis that contains the testicles.

Self-Worth/Self-Esteem: An individual's overall emotional evaluation of their own worth. Self-worth is both a judgment of the self and an attitude toward the self. More generally, the term is used to describe a confidence in one's own value or abilities.

Semen: The male reproductive fluid, which contains spermatozoa in suspension. Semen exits the penis through ejaculation.

Serial Monogamy: A mating system in which a man or woman can only form a long-term, committed relationship (such as marriage) with one partner at a time. Should the relationship dissolve, the individual may go on to form another relationship, but only after the first relationship has ceased.

Sex (Sexual Intercourse): Sexual activity, also known as coitus or copulation, which is most commonly understood to refer to the insertion of the penis into the vagina (vaginal sex). It should be noted that there are a wide range of various sexual activities and the boundaries of what constitutes sexual intercourse are still under debate. See also, intercourse.

Sexting: The sending or distribution of sexually explicit images, messages, or other material via phones, email, or instant messaging.

Sexual Abuse: The improper sexual usage or treatment of another person, often to unfairly gain power or other benefit in the relationship. In instances of sexual abuse, undesired sexual behaviors are forced upon one person by another.

Sexual Assault: A term often used in legal contexts to refer to sexual violence. Sexual assault occurs when there is any non-consensual sexual contact or violence. Examples include rape, groping, forced kissing, child sexual abuse, and sexual torture.

Sexual Harassment: Harassment involving unwanted sexual advances or obscene remarks. Sexual harassment can be a form of sexual coercion as well as an undesired sexual proposition, including the promise of reward in exchange for sexual favors.

Sexual Identification: How one thinks of oneself in terms of whom one is romantically or sexually attracted to.

Shame: The painful feeling arising from the consciousness of something dishonorable, improper, ridiculous, etc., done by oneself or another.

Slut-shaming: The act of criticizing, attacking, or shaming a woman for her real or presumed sexual activity, or for behaving in ways that someone thinks are associated with her real or presumed sexual activity.

Sperm: The male reproductive cell, consisting of a head, midpiece, and tail. The head contains the genetic material, while the tail is used to propel the sperm as it travels towards the egg.

Spontaneous Erection: A penile erection that occurs as an automatic response to a variety of stimuli, some of which is sexual and some of which is physiological.

STD: An abbreviation that refers to sexually transmitted diseases, many of which persist in the body for life. These are illnesses that are communicable through sexual behaviors, including intercourse. Some of these illnesses can also be transmitted through contact with various bodily fluids.

STI: An abbreviation that refers to sexually transmitted infections. These are illnesses that are communicable through sexual behaviors, including intercourse. Some of these illnesses can be transmitted through blood contact. Not all STI's lead to a disease and become an STD.

Straight: A slang term for heterosexuality, a sexual orientation in which one is attracted to members of the opposite sex (males are attracted to females; females are attracted to males). See also, heterosexual.

Syphilis: Syphilis is an infection typically spread through sexual contact. It is a chronic, contagious, usually venereal and often congenital disease. If left untreated, syphilis can produce chancres, rashes, and systemic lesions in a clinical course with three stages continued over many years.

Test Touch: Seemingly innocent touches by a predator or offender, such as a pat on the back or a squeeze on the arm, that are meant to normalize kids to being in physical contact with the predator. Test touches can quickly progress from these innocent touches to more dangerous and damaging ones.

Testicles: The male gonad, which is located inside the scrotum beneath the penis. The testicles are responsible for the production of sperm and androgens, primarily testosterone.

Transgender: A condition or state in which one's physical sex does not match one's perceived gender identity. A transgender individual may have been assigned a sex at birth based on their genitals, but feel that this assignment is false or incomplete. They also may be someone who does not wish to be identified by conventional gender roles and instead combines or moves between them (often referred to as gender-fluid).

Uncomfortable: Feeling or causing discomfort or unease; disquieting.

Under the Influence: Being physically affected by alcohol or drugs.

Urethra: The tube that connects the urinary bladder to the urinary meatus (the orifice through which the urine exits the urethra tube). In males, the urethra runs down the penis and opens at the end of the penis. In females, the urethra is internal and opens between the clitoris and the vagina.

Urination: The process through which urine is released from the urinary bladder to travel down the urethra and exit the body at the urinary meatus.

Uterus: A major reproductive sex organ in the female body. The uterus is located in the lower half of the torso, just above the vagina. It is the site in which offspring are conceived and in which they gestate during pregnancy.

Vagina: The muscular tube leading from the external genitals to the cervix of the uterus in women. During sexual intercourse, the penis can be inserted into the vagina. During childbirth, the infant exits the uterus through the vagina.

Vaginal Discharge/Secretions: Vaginal discharge is the umbrella term for the clear/milky white fluid that secretes from the vagina daily. This discharge is the means by which the vagina keeps itself clean by discharging cells and debris. When a woman is sexually aroused, she will see an increase in this secretion as a means of preparing the vagina for sex.

Vaginal Sex: A form of sexual intercourse in which the penis is inserted into the vagina.

Vaginismus: A medical condition in which a woman experiences pain from any form of vaginal penetration, including sexual intercourse, the use of tampons or menstrual cups, and/or gynecological examinations.

Victim: A person who is harmed, injured, or killed as the result of an accident or crime.

Virgin: A person, male or female, who has never engaged in sexual intercourse.

Vulva: The parts of the female sexual organs that are on the outside of the body.

Wet Dreams: A slang term for nocturnal emissions. A nocturnal emission is a spontaneous orgasm that occurs during sleep. Nocturnal emissions can occur in both males (ejaculation) and females (lubrication of the vagina).

CHECK OUT ALL OF OUR BOOKS AVAILABLE ON OUR WEBSITE AND AMAZON.COM

Conversations With My Kids: 30 Essential Family Discussions for the Digital Age

Parenting in the digital age has never been tougher. The world is changing faster than we can keep up with! It seems like there's always a new toy or device at every turn. With all this new tech, comes new information and new dangers. Our kids are exploring world issues and personal questions you and I didn't face at their age. Conversations With My Kids gives you the words and handy discussion questions to have meaningful talks about 30 very timely topics.

How to Talk to Your Kids About Pornography: 2nd Edition

Never before has it been so easy to talk with your children or teens about this tough topic. With smartphones and tablets everywhere, our kids are engaged in one of the most incredible social experiments ever conceived in the history of mankind. Within this alarming experiment, our children are becoming entrenched in an increasingly pornified culture. Take the time now to protect and prepare your family. Whether they are 6 or 16, you will have worthwhile, relevant discussions that will educate and prepare your family. Also available in Spanish.

30 Days of Sex Talks Empowering Your Child with Knowledge of Sexual Intimacy

Written by parents and reviewed by professionals, 30 Days of Sex Talks makes it simple for you and your child to talk about the mechanics of sex, emotional intimacy, healthy and abusive relationships, and so much more. We've broken down "the talk" into 30 uncomplicated "chats" to make it simple for you to engage in these critical conversations with your children. Remember, talking to your kids about healthy sexuality doesn't have to be awkward! It can be very empowering for you and your kids.

30 Days to a Stronger Child

As our families face an uncertain future, there are skills and qualities we must help our children develop in order for them to grow resilient, strong, and successful. That's why we've given you an engaging, straightforward way to teach the vital concepts of physical health, emotional strength, social skills, spiritual balance, and intellectual growth to your children. We've included activities, discussions, and questions that will empower you to raise a stronger, more exceptional child.

Petra's Power to See: A Media Literacy Adventure

We are surrounded by messages (media)—most of them are beautiful! Some inspire us to learn and grow, but some messages are empty and unhealthy. Join Petra and her dad as they venture into the city to learn about the powerful media messages all around us. They come face to face with clear and hidden messages in different media such as advertising, social media, and fake news. Petra and her dad will teach you what media is, how it affects us, and how to make wise choices when using media.

Noah's New Phone: A Story About Using Technology for Good

When Noah gets a smartphone for his birthday, he quickly realizes the power he holds in his hands. He becomes aware of its power to do good and inspire positive change as well as its negative and hurtful capacity. A great read-together book, Noah's New Phone also includes a handy workbook to reinforce important elements of the story like choices, safety, healthy boundaries and the huge potential within technology.

Messages About Me: Sydney's Story: A Girl's Journey to Healthy Body Image

Messages About Me: Wade's Story: A Boy's Quest for Healthy Body Image

Our kids receive hundreds, possibly thousands of messages every day from friends, family members, acquaintances, advertisements, social media, TV, and elsewhere. Join Sydney and Wade on their individual journeys as they first struggle and then, with the help of parents and a good friend, come to understand they are happy to be themselves and are truly beautiful the way they are.

EDUCATEEMPOWERKIDS

IF YOU ENJOYED THIS BOOK, PLEASE LEAVE A POSITIVE REVIEW ON AMAZON.COM

Subscribe to our websites for exclusive offers and information,

www.educateempowerkids.org

Be sure to check out our accompanying video series for this book at educateempowerkids.org

To view or download the additional resources listed at the end of each lesson, please follow the link in this QR code.

Made in the USA
Las Vegas, NV
27 February 2024

86405828R00063